Connecticut River Review

Connecticut River Review
2022

dedicated to the memory of David K. Leff

Connecticut River Review is a national poetry journal sponsored by the Connecticut Poetry Society. All rights revert to the authors on publication.

Editors: Ginny Lowe Connors, Debbie Gilbert, and Luisa Caycedo-Kimura
Additional Readers: Antoinette Brim-Bell and Aaron Caycedo-Kimura
Design: Cindy Stewart
Cover Photo by Dorothea Oldani on Unsplash

ISBN: 978-0-9785382-9-3

Contents

POEMS

PRIZE WINNERS

Liz Abrams-Morley

Olivia and I Learn About the Nature of Time and Space

Not the shortest day, Olivia corrects,
time is all the same, the days,
I mean. She's reaching for words

to encapsulate what yogis and physicists,
even visionaries can't articulate,
but she doesn't know that yet,

seven years old, maybe eight, a so-large block
of her school life to date spent in a square box
trying to learn science via Zoom

in this season of plague. What must she feel, Olivia,
ten months away from playmates, such dark times,
everything askew? Cold solstice and I learn

Jupiter and Saturn align as light wanes, *one great*
conjunction of the two largest planets in our known system
combining their brightness over a tired city.

Just look south and west, Corina instructs
as I sit on my yoga mat what we call *hours* later.
There will be such brightness, and is this

irony or blessing on a day when most of the hours
all days contain will be spent in darkness
before the world tilts back. In second grade,

I learned only of time's forward motion, learned
never to hold still in the now as now, nearing seventy,
I hold still, this Great Conjunction glimmering.

Brian Wallace Baker

Henbit in Spring

Cold raindrops
offer themselves generously
to my skin and squinting eyes,

then—

       a sudden cessation,

and I see our bedroom window aglow. Somewhere in that second-story
apartment my little family waits for me to return from the dumpster.
My whole existence fits within 600 square feet. Despite toddler clutter
and clatter, it's a good place, but we were grateful last Sunday for the
respite of a country drive. Our bodies opened to the opening of the
world as we drove through purple fields of pinprick flowers, millions
of them, each cluster a life rooted to its place, to the nourishing soul of
the soil. To these plants the world is infinite, and even the sun-bleached
barns wilting by the roadside can't comprehend its generations,

nor can we, blooming
in this fragrant universe,
so well fed

for this

       brief spring.

Sherri Bedingfield

Broad-Winged Katydid Calls in September

A night song, it clicks with crispy sounds, a raspy whisper.
A future mate listens with her whole body somewhere
in a haven of darkness. Acorns and narrow-leafed maple seeds
collect everywhere trees are.

Branches swell with seeds that dive, spin as helicopters do,
float like feathers—twirl, drift, rest briefly under mother trees—
if earth hasn't grounded them at the edge of a half-buried stone,
or tucked a few under thick-bladed grass, they lift, dry as air—
fly and fall again.

Katydid's delicate wings are veined like maple leaves,
its grassy green body like a long new maple seed. Its night calls
are deeper than the cricket's bell-chirp.

All day katydid shelters, invisible, tucked into shrubs and trees.
It eats pointed maple leaves in the dark, until time
for singing.

If you were able to see its face, its tiny red tongue,
quick black eyes, elegant legs; long and stilted,
a whisper for wings—katydid moves as dancer—its beauty
could still you, take your breath.

Erica Bernheim

The Cadaver Dog Speaks

While they are still hopeful, I lead
them. Any outcome can be a good boy.
If we find something, they'll know.

If we find nothing, hope (linen-
scented, we flannel homewards)
clutches their fingers and yet points

me forward in dreams. I pull them
through the fields of their intuitions,
through the lies that preserve both

the living and their dead. One type
of lie preserves a body, the other sub-
consumes it. Nose dipped to this ground,

I lead them through the shimmy of each
field. I control this walk. The case files
lag behind. Some nights, each sewer

houses its own set of eyes. We find
people twisted raw with suspicions.
These were people who rode horses.

They lived in houses. They will confess
on courthouse steps. They will fight
so hard to stay part of a world that

clearly, badly, no longer wanted them in it.

Nick Bertelson

Didus Ineptus Abecedarian

All that remains: a hollow skull, keelless breastbones,
            bits and pieces scavenged from pits where we
cooked you over open flames, and that nickname: Dodo
Does it say more about you or us?
                        Even your taxonomy
feels like an insult: Latin: *in* "not," *aptus* "fit."

Granted a name so damning,
        how could you not become a self-fulfilling prophecy?
It's one thing to have wings for vanity's sake

                        (Judge not, lest ye be judged.)

Knowing all we do, though, it's hard to pity a bird so
lazy she surrendered her flight to wind.

Mauritius harbored few predators, however—
            no mongooses or monkeys ogling your eggs,
only ocean winds ruffling your feathers.

Paradise is the kingdom of the just. It simply never lasts
quite long enough. So tell us, were those Dutch clippers

                redolent of apocalyptic horsemen, or could you even
see them through the jungle scrub?

    Tell us, do future species joke about going the way of the human?

Under different circumstances, we may have
vouched for you. Instead, we picked our teeth
with your bones. We laughed at your
            xiphi-beaks, your hopeless fledglings,
your petulant wails like children screaming.

                Zeniths, you've told us, require no sky.

11

Laura Bonazzoli

Early Morning, Beauchamp Point

All night
the sea sang
surging to crescendo in the shoreline hollows then
drawing back its cords of sky
to surge again.

It sang
while gulls cried
while pods of dolphins whistled to their young even
while silent kelp and coral formed and died
and long before land came forth

from its womb.
Scientists think the oceans formed
four billion years ago as vapors from our globe of magma
rose into the atmosphere then cooled and began
to fall as rain.

The rain fell
for thousands of years and covered the molten Earth with sea.
More years passed. Fins became limbs and gills became lungs and
ears and now some would say they hear
in the song of the sea

a promise of eternity. But I
take off my shoes and close my eyes and dream
I hear our ancient mother singing to awaken me to this brief
morning and my place
in this brief world.

Laura Bonazzoli

Evening of PM2.5

Particulate matter is composed of liquid droplets and inhalable particles, such as from soot or smoke. The particles of PM2.5 have a diameter of 2.5 micrometers or smaller.

Our weather apps flash the warning:
AQI orange: unhealthy for sensitive groups.
We go online. It's PM2.5
from the wildfires. NOAA has video.
We watch the smoke drift

two thousand miles east.
At sunset we climb Amsbury Hill, view
boats chugging in brown haze,
islands dulled like dusty birds
waiting for rain.

We are all members of sensitive groups
irrevocably. Now
as PM2.5 fills the sacs of our lungs,
we watch the red-phosphorus moon
strike the rim of sea and imagine

by the smoggy beach,
cattails and sea peas,
crabs and fish and ospreys,
moths and pollen-laden bees
sluggish in the heavy night.

I reach out my hand.
You take it,

let it go.
Tonight we'll dream our lives
break apart like glaciers, wake
in ruddy darkness, wander rooms
gathering ash.

Michael McKeown Bondhus

Desire, Pennsylvania

> *desire is full*
> *of endless distances*
> *—Robert Hass*

Across fields of soybeans
in the small red town
in southern Pennsylvania
fieldworkers labor in the mud
exactly one mile from the Methodist Church
where the preacher speaks to the farmers on Sundays
of resurrection-time and the titillations of heaven.

Fifty feet above the altar there's a mural
where cherubs fly on cracked wings,
blowing tarnished trumpets
to honor a yellowing Jesus.

Just as far as the church but in the opposite direction,
the Gentleman's Club, sagging beneath
the weight of six days' desire,
frowns every day but Saturday,
when the girls take to the stage,
dancing for tips under
violet lights, stern as schoolmarms
and unapproachable as angels.

From across the highway, the workers' heads line up
flat against the sky
while their bellies and belt lines crop
tight to the ground,
dreaming of weekends
spent with two desires
disparate as sky and soil,
their endless attempts to close an unending distance.

Roxanne Cardona

Tethered to Little Feet

after Grace Schulman

Willet, Leggett, Barretto, Edgewater, East Bronx—
those whispered t's that clip the tongue.

Best Bet Auto Glass, Bruckner moves, bare bottoms
shake the Badabing club, the ladies strutting

Tiffany Street hard when the moon slices our East
River into threes, a sharp display of twinkling

gold and pinks. There's Tami, in silver-inched-
heels, must poke holes in the dark carpet of her

new John's *semi.* Her purple sequined fingers
raised in prayer, as if to say—*God save me, tonight.*

At dawn, the red ball rises raw atop
the Corpus Christi Monastery, the nuns black

with forgiveness. The produce trucks plow across
Hunts Street, spitting out gas like gunshot blasts

or timbales tuned high on Barretto Point Park.
Locals gather round the hoop, where copper-

colored basketballs are jammed by young
muscled arms, sparkling wet in tints

of chocolate, amber, and toast. Way up
Spofford Avenue Hill, there is a scene

I could watch forever: Over-sized backpacks
tethered to pairs of little feet, talking too loud,

running to school, impossibly late.
Where I will always wait for them.

Susana H. Case

The Erasure

I want to tell you about my abortion,
about vacuum pumps, blood, the whole
buzz-killer event, but all I say is,
I'm feeling a little off, just want to sleep,

sheets stretched tight and welcoming.
Maybe I'll see you tomorrow, lover
rejected, flower closing for the night.
I want to say something deep about loss,

how I'll likely cry over it, and us,
twenty years from now, especially
during holidays, when I'm most likely
to ask myself, *what did I do—*

rhetorical. But probably I'd be crying
procedure or not, the number of times
I've seen motherhood not work out: child
living under a bridge, child perpetually angry,

child done talking, child slamming head
into a wall again and again.
My breasts are still sore to remind me.
I want to say, *please stay with me,*

and then I don't. The erasure was
so quick, it seems to have hardly happened.
I'm not sure I like you that much.
If I tell you, if you stay with me, today is real.

Lucia Cherciu

Synesthesia

In the time to write this poem
an animal disappears from the earth, extinct.

Who decides which artists become famous,
whose art survives through centuries?

Somebody made costumes for a play
that has closed because of the pandemic.

Somebody looks through the clothes of the departed
sorting what to keep, what to give away.

In the time to write this poem
a child cries while revising her Monday essay

and the mother bakes a pie to cheer her up,
so the child connects writing with baking,

the bubbly color of raspberries with the perfume
of having finished a task she abhors.

When she completes the essay, the child
reads out loud about extinct animals.

A vegetarian, she vows to save the planet,
protect animals. Somewhere,

villagers throw away garbage into the creek.
A company disposes of toxic refuse into the river.

The child watches a blue jay in the maple tree,
learns of horrors inflicted to the earth,

homework obviating the need for change,
burdening her with loss and guilt.

Paula Colangelo

My Father's Autopsy

What we learned
you didn't know yourself—

enlarged prostate, swollen heart,
aneurysm that claimed you.

What we learned
I didn't know when I found you.

Your clothes set out for the next
workday when the sound of collapse

drew me in to check. I was younger
than my youngest child is now

unaware I couldn't save you
as I stumbled to recall CPR.

Forgot to tilt head back, check airway.
It took years to believe there was nothing

I could have done. A pre-med friend
once invited me to see the cadavers.

Smell of formaldehyde, cool air
and rows of white cloth.

She said it was important for people
to respect the deceased who gave their bodies

to science. And so many years later I do—
I think of the woman with breast cancer,

the man with cirrhosis, nameless but willing
to bare their injury under light.

Robert Cording

Composition in Orange, Yellow and Blue

Up early, I'm looking for a fresh start,
anything to brighten my day
or at least ward off the lackluster
sense of something always missing
(or is it me missing something?).
The sun rises above the double-wides
that rim the man-made pond
where patches of steam clouds hover
over the water and a few of the ugliest turtles—
Florida soft shells—up-periscope
their reptilian noses. There are bundles
of shingles stacked a few feet apart
on the unshingled roof across the water
when the roofers arrive in their beaten-up trucks
and simply go about business,
the day starting as they climb their ladders,
fit and nail down the drip edge,
their air guns rat-tat-tatting,
before it's straight on to the first course
of shingles with that unselfconscious know-how
of workers who do the same thing every day.

Dressed in orange T-shirts, their heads
are wrapped in yellow and blue bandanas
as if the roof were a desert border they had to cross
by the end of this already blistering day.
I watch them on and off, their stick-to-it,
no-nonsense attitude, their brown skin glistening
with sweat. Then the equipoise of noon.
Lunch in the house's shadows, and in the hours
after, the men slowing down, then galvanizing
last-push efforts as the sun relents
and prepares to take its daily plunge
in the Gulf. At last, they are done.
One, still on the roof, looks it over
with justifiable pride, or just enjoys the view

from up there. I doubt he can see Rookery Bay,
but maybe, and *enjoyment* may be
too strong a word for what he's feeling,
or maybe the wrong word entirely
for the difficult history he's most likely living.
What can I know? Still, I'm enjoying
the way he straddles the roof's peak,
relaxed, as if after a day's climb he'd reached
the evening's little waystation,
his orange shirt blazing, tomorrow's job
just over the horizon but not here yet.

Robert Cording

Rhinella Marina

Not the basso profundo of a bullfrog's
jug-a-rum, but the fusillade of a woodpecker
"on steroids," Google informs me
regarding the caterwaul of what I now know
to be the Bufos outside my window.

Invasive, they've overrun southern Florida.
A full moon eggs them on, excess
their norm. There's just no *enough*
with these toads. When I go outside to look
with a flashlight, I come upon

a six-inch one, all warts and poisonous glands,
that keeps up its drumming, an epic
of sexual hunger that seems fitting,
and somehow, in this deranged night,
akin to the blinking red cell tower

that carries the frenzy of our calls
pinging from one tower to another
as we project our desires.
I intend to live forever, or die trying,
Groucho quipped, and this free-for-all is

relentless, as if these toads were aware,
as Groucho was, of the fixed hours
we all get, and of the hurry they produce,
forcing me to see that self-poisoning self,
feverish for only another tomorrow.

Jennifer Cox

Spring Baby

The 100-year flood started
Between her legs, belly swollen
Waters broken, flash flooding
The husband with a mop
Signaling the imminent arrival
That spring was late and
Baby right on time, forty weeks to the day
On his entrance, screaming
At the injustice of birth

After, amniotic fluid poured down
As rain from the sky
Filling the Ottawa, Rideau
Flowing the news to every home:
"New life is here"
        Along the riverbank
Friends and family brought
Sandbags, to celebrate the baby

In the 100-year flood
New parents inundated with
The responsibility of spring

Oluwasegun Isaac Daramola

ode to the poem lost to the beautiful darkness

any minute now, and the light I glorify will go off,
and darkness will ravage, again, and the eyes
will settle for uncertain hours, and the mouth
will repeat verses because the mental sketch
of the poem must not be forgotten, and the ink
will be useless on paper because even if a candle
cannot escape from my table, the matchstick
will not be found, and the wardrobe will be stocked
with shirts of bold creases, and there will be no music
because the player will be down, and I will lose the verses
of the poem, word by word from the end,
because the brain will spark my being
and it will lose its efficiency in doing so,
and I will lose the last stanza of this poem
because it will be impossible to make music
out of what I no longer know,
and because the cricket's song, like pain,
will fill my hearing, and the sullen loss of a poem
will continue, morpheme after morpheme,
melting out of my understanding, and any second
now, soon, the last morpheme of this poem
that laced my lips will also peel into darkness,
because the dark felt more beautiful

Annie Diamond

Birds of the Midwest

At the Indiana Dunes Visitor Center
I get a deck of cards that features

54 of the most compelling Midwest birds.
Their names so metrical and full

of fashion: white throated, rose breasted, red
shouldered. I never thought of bird shoulders.

I like the *Indigo Bunting* and the *Common Loon*
best for names, though—looking at the former,

I think of flags and parades, festive plastic.
Common Latinate, *Loon* Germanic: these

twin kings of English adorn the king
of diamonds. I touch Lake Michigan

at the Indiana lakeshore: so blue and temperate.
Looking west I can see downtown Chicago even

without glasses on. I love the *Northern Flicker*
too, on the five of clubs: a kind of woodpecker,

one of few that migrates.

Marc Alan Di Martino

Neanderthals

On learning that Neanderthals made art

My DNA is part-Neanderthal
I marvel as an unexpected jab
of pride waltzes into my bloodstream.

How cavalier I've always been to mock
their oversized skulls and poor manners.
Here on evolution's road-to-nowhere

they lumber far-off in the rearview mirror
behind us, the once-and-future royalty
of the Darwinian Olympic Games,

supreme despots of a rocky outpost.
Our reptile egos slithering within
we can't quite forgive the Neanderthals

for not being, well, *us.* They're catching up,
however. A splatter of red paint
on a cave wall becomes a symbol, a cipher,

a scepter we thought was ours alone to wield.
Now it's the bread that we must break with them—
begrudgingly, as if it were citizenship

or a ballot in our upcoming elections.
What right on earth do we have to be us,
anyway? We might so easily have been them.

Thomas Festa

Bending the Light

Ishiguro says nostalgia
is to the emotions what
idealism is to the intellect.

(A son's half-smile
as he waits
on the broken
sidewalk for
the bus before
the first day of kindergarten.)

(A daughter's look
of distracted pleasure
when she plays
through a piece
on the piano
for the first time.)

Gather these
moments, I tell myself,
the way rain beads
on a cuticle
of waxy leaf
so the plant retains water

enough to spite
the arid climate.
Those droplets show
the world
beyond them.
Through its

latticed
honeycombs, frost
collects the dawn.

James Finnegan

Gatling

that is, as in the gun, the first real machine gun…
It's said he'd regretted that he was known more
for that hand-cranked instrument of mass death
than for the seed drill. Isn't it always seeds versus
bullets on this earth? Robert Jordan Gatling,
a man who because of an outbreak of smallpox
became a doctor. A man who patented many things,
improved many things, like bicycles and toilets,
who in his lifetime made and lost a few fortunes.
In his latter years, formed a company to manufacture
steam ploughs. Those machines too would have come
in handy at Chickamauga, at Shiloh, or Gettysburg,
all those fallen bodies, arrayed in rows, the sun
on them, needing to be ploughed under.

Marsha Foss

"Why Am I Telling You All This?"

last line from a poem by Virginia Hamilton Adair

Listen, old woman,
    you who brushed ants from the melon
    so you could savor life to the very end,

those tiny insects, "wild for their melon toddies"
    were no more eager to drink and be drunk on the sweetness
    in their life than you were in yours.

Tell me, when the children came,
    were your days so full with chaotic picnics and play
    that there was nothing to do but relish the rich luscious fare?

And when your husband ended it all, did you
    think about your grandmothers
    decorating wreaths with black ribbons on doors

for their own husbands now dead?
    They, who carried black-edged handkerchiefs
    and wrote on notepaper with borders of black,

still danced and were merry, you say.
    Did you, like them, dance and cry with laughter
    while sipping the bitter flavor of loss?

Or was life too succulent and ripe even then
    to stop to wipe the juice from your hands and mouth?
    Did the world taste different after that?

Was your appetite dimmed as your eyes failed
    and you wrote in utter darkness?
    Were you despairing

or could you still taste the fruit of your work,
     still feel the melon's rough rind,
     still smell the mellow fragrance in old age?

How did you tell me so much?

Note: Virginia Hamilton Adair was 83 when her first book of poems, *Ants on the Melon*, was published in 1996, though she had been writing all her life. Her second book came out in 1998. She died in 2004 at the age of 91.

Jennifer L. Freed

What to Do When You See Why Your Daughter Wears Long Sleeves

Gather all the pieces. Hold
tight. Breathe.
Know
that you will fall
apart
again.

Hand her over
to the firm-voiced therapist
the way you gave her to the surgeon when she was seven—
full of hope
and helplessness, trusting the blade
against her skin.

Wait.

Follow her lead.

Don't think it will help to hide your knives. You will not stop her
need.

Use all your strength to believe
this will not kill her.

Forgive her
when she cannot
explain.

Someday she may tell you
frayed skin helps her
not to hear the goblins—the clicking
of their tongues.

Hope
that one day
she will wrap her lips around their taunts
and suck
the strength from them
and spit
the venom out.

Jennifer L. Freed

What I Don't Say to the Bleeding Girl When I Give Her a Blank Book

Write your bones
out from under the bed.
Write the goblin chant.
Write yourself falling
through darkness.
Listen.
You will hear doors.
You will hide.
There are so many ways
to hide.
Write the smile guarding your eyes.
Open one door
if you can.
Don't stop
what comes. You can cut,
if you need to, later.
For now, this
is your out. Write
the leap and the snarl.
Write the edge
of the voice in your hand.
No one need see
what you hurl at the page.
You can kill it,
if you like,
once you've brought it to light.

Louis Gabordi

Shadow Orchard

> *The shadow orchard is the name given to fruit bearing trees*
> *found growing outside the cultivated orchard.*
>   —Jim Chapman, The Shadow Orchard

This is where the orchard would have been,
sloping from the lichen-dappled boulders to its north,
warming in the slant of morning sun that would have filled
this patch of land if I had cleared it.

I thought I'd keep a dozen apples,
a pair of quinces for the calm that quaintness brings me,
and a couple seckel pears, such as those I climbed
along the sandy driveway of my childhood.

By now the trees would have been bearing fruit for decades,
and I would have a chair or two within them
where I could catch the sun or shade as I preferred
while sitting with my coffee and the morning's reading.

In my later years, I would have been a slow sentry
pausing at each tree, twirling silken tents around a stick
and dropping pests into a soapy bucket.
With so few trees, my vigilance may have been enough.

Even to myself at times, I would have made excuses
for wandering the hundred feet or so just to be among them,
to sit and follow bees, honeyed sparks against the sun,
rising from the cups of pale blossoms.

And when I'd passed, from time to time my family
may have gathered in the fragrance of the gnarled branches
and thought of me, and spoken of how deeply
I had loved this place of peace.

Margaret Gibson

It Was Like This

It was like this—
in the crowded restaurant
you sat across from me at a table
loud with mutual friends
and strangers, you were
a stranger, and after a while
I looked directly into your eyes
and asked, "Who are you?"
without knowing I was sitting
only a table's width
from the rest of my life,
how could I have known that?
And in the hum of conversation
and the clink of wine glasses,
in the chaos of laughter
and unacknowledged pain,
the rest of my life said softly,
as if the stars we were born under
had conferred and agreed:
"We will make up for it.
Sometimes you will eat fresh
figs and cheeses, sometimes
a mustard seed of the unknown,
but we will make up for it.
From now on, the rain
will be a scrim of bright beads
on a branch of the morning
as sun through the window
brightens the bed covers,
spreading over your bodies
as they rise and fall and fold
into each other. And yes,
there will be blues
and botheration—but a part
of you mute for decades
will speak in a new language

of pure wildness and gladness—
don't be afraid." This is what
I heard that night in the crowded
restaurant, across the table,
before either of us had realized
that the rest of a life could be
embodied, then offered
all at once, offered and received
suddenly in a shudder of breath.

Margaret Gibson

Letter to Rakusan

20 March 2020

Officially it's spring now in the woods
and, according to the genii of this old wood

house, it's spring when I see the phoebes back,
ready to nest where the bend in the gutter pipe backs

into a sheltered corner. Spring also, if here and there,
because wild onions spring up here and there

in clumps and patches—and like an old god's green
stubble, garden chives poke through. I green

as I relate these comings and goings on the wild earth
to you, brother Rakusan, who live on the earth

at a juncture whose mountains and wild rivers
brush up against each other, the rivers

made of no snow, no ice, only the rush and hush
of the tumble-down, resounding hush

monks know when they sit in stillness, or in stillness
go full tilt at their chores. In stillness

at my daily chore of word-work, I join you
dear friend, more fully here for knowing that you

who also sit and work, doing nothing, are
there. Broken couplets, spare verse—these are

the elusive ways I partner with emptiness. And yes,
slowly I come to it: old age, sickness, and yes

death, as they make their way rapidly across
the earth, virus by virus, and no begging bowl, no cross,

no altar, no zabuton or zafu, halts it. I go outside to stay
in. I stay in, and go deeper in, to stay

abreast of the phoebe's tail-wag, the up-down flick
that may be nothing at all, or merely a fleck

of motion out the corner of my eye. At that point
of motion, spring gathers into a still point

in the heart of change, the forsythia I love
burning gold on its blossoming whips. The man I love

is new to this house, but an old familiar in my heart,
as old as spring itself, its old and new wild hart

thirsting, just as poetry thirsts, and nothing,
nothing slakes it. Dear Rakusan, your name has *nothing*

in it. *Raku* means *no*. I'm wind and stream's no wind,
no stream, sending you these words on a path of no wind

as it goes everywhere: bringing with it everything
and nothing…spring.

Cindy Glovinsky

Holy Week at Work

This is holy week,
which I'm celebrating by listening with headphones
to the Fauré Requiem while proofreading a paper
on smoking rates in China

when my best friend Bonnie sends me an email
fuming about having to move to a different cubicle,
and I send her my poem about office bullies
and suggest that she quit DTE and join the Peace Corps

and the choir is up to the Kyrie as I read
that the smoking rates have gone down
because people in China really are smoking less,
and not just because of the changes in age structure

and Bonnie says she can't possibly join the Peace Corps
because she can't leave her sister who has lung cancer,
and I'm looking at the smoking paper references,
which will take me at least an hour to redo,

and now the baritone is bellowing
libera me, libera me from the grave
and I remember that this week is also Passover
and I want to listen, but just then

Rhonda comes fussing in
about some account sheet or other,
and I say some words to make her go away
and she does,

and then for a moment
I sit breathing and listening.

When I look back up at the screen
I see that the author has already fixed
all the references herself in the pdf,

and there's another email from Bonnie
about the swamp cabbage and butterflies
she saw on her seven-mile hike,
and all the soprano souls
are floating up over the world
along with the butterflies,
like cigarette smoke
wafting all the way
from China.

Kristina Hakanson

Gloaming

Let me tell you why I walk toward darkness
on the asphalt between rows of five-unit buildings
& it might seem like I go nowhere in particular

& that's probably true—but the light changes so fast, so much.
The sky's palette settles down for the night like pebbles
sinking into the sea. Brown tree trunks submerge,

penumbra speaks to shadow, nightjars & bats transform
as silhouettes. The sun herself congeals to a deep red wound
which the night invisible's tongs cauterize.

The day splits itself from night the way nature cleaves
her atoms to create something new, the sky's way of becoming indigo,
maybe what the angel saw on his great whoosh to the floor.

Tires & engines fade, the breeze shushes—so you see,
nothing is special except the words that make it so
during these minutes of witness on this crepuscular stroll

which might as well be the candle lit to mark the holy day
or the blowing out of the wishing candle on the cake
or the extinguishing of a cigarette by eighty-something Rex

who lives in the apartment above ours. He's now climbing his stairs
after a smoke, just like he did last night & the night before—
not a test of oxygen but a testament of time. I'm almost back

inside, where my collar will carry the scents of earth & water
from deep underground, the affair of how night shades
itself into our own shadows already forgotten.

Paul Hamill

Paean to Country Dust

City folks think dust is marginal:
A problem of finding tolerable levels,
As with traffic jams. But on the farm
You see the grand and dreary permanence
Of the drizzle of chaffs, molds, insect remnants,
Pollens, blown soil—matter without form
As before creation. The skin of everything
Sheds. On the farm pond a fine sheen
Sinks at your coming footstep or the plop of a frog
While high above earth's surface flows of dust
Are rivers in air's ocean, storms
Of infinitesimals sifting to pile new deserts
On old, seed snow, and sink the pyramids.

Consider that you always work for dust.
I don't just mean our personal drift to clay
That as the poet says, will plug a cask:
Dust is the one sure product of our labor,
Entropic freight of construction sites, thin bloom
Above the plow that breaks dry ground for flowers:
Amorphously a record, highlight, and veil.
Any morning of life you know beforehand
There's one work that you'll leave unformed,
One consequence you can't design or steer,
One layer of weariness already blurring words
The moving finger of time won't blot but dust will:
The human shadows in the nuclear flash,
The changeless prophecy of the changing wind.

Shellie Harwood

Lost in Sweet Aleppo

Your mother's body was washed
by you and your sister,
wrapped in four pieces of Damascus linen
for the burial.
Your hands are raw when you return to me.

Your face is a hard stone, eyes dark and dry,
heart clenched in your teeth.
I pool oils in my palm to warm them,
I knead your aching hands.

Tell me about your home, I say to you.
Say what you have lost.
You say your mother is a lamp gone out,
you swallow her name. You speak instead
of the cat man of Aleppo,
who stayed behind to tend the rubble
and the orphan cats when Aleppo fell.
The more he feeds, the more they multiply.
No one returns to claim the ghosts he saves.

You shed tears only for a lone bald ibis called Zenobia,
who has not been told of her own extinction,
and searches all of Syria for one to love.
There is no music now. She knows no song.

For every grain of sand,
there are ten thousand stars, you say to me.
You can see them all from sweet Aleppo,
now that the lights are gone.

Judd Hess

Joshua Tree

O, but the dry earth does not grow Ahab's whiskers.
It sports the whale's harpoons.

I learned this sea-truth
on the third night lost upon the Mojave
    beyond the old silver-mine shafts
    deep-drowned in rust-water,
head-heavy on the vagabond sand
    among quartzite and gneiss.

In this gray world,
    bleak as the sea,
                what stands straight in the desert
        as I have tried to stand,
          branching skyward,
        invoking aid of alliance like Moses
                    with raised fist;
          what might have stood glorious
as apocalypse—fire on the stormy yardarm—
    the death-drive defiant as Jezebel—

fails, as I did. I'm sorry. I lost you
the second night, punching gray
    as rope might for rust-water, as
    vengeance might the sea itself
with a sharp stick, hoping to poke purpose
    from quartzite and gneiss.

O Love, there is no tree on this sea:
only the flagging stab of a wobbly grave cross.

Maggie Rue Hess

Correspondence

I

We wrote letters for the better part of three years. You can't replace the feeling of a pen in hand, of mail on the way; you can get creative with the contents. What we sent back and forth: sketches, restaurant napkins, explications, sauce stains, photos, extra stickers. Once, I sent him a picture of a can, pull tab opened, revealing a second lid, still sealed. It said, "Getting to know me is like," though eventually it wasn't true. The small room of the page is all doors and only one ear. It was his, so I trusted it. The quiet microphone of the page chooses its audience. That was me for him. Our families fell apart but we knitted them into sentences and held ourselves together. We did not agree on the most beautiful part of a pregnant woman – I still think it's the subtle notice of her belly button. What we sent back and forth: all the ways to tell a friend *I miss you* just short of saying *I need you in my life*. How would he know me if I had no paper? Doesn't matter. Now I forget the numbers on his street, nevermind the zip code. We sent letters, but now we don't.

II

We wrote letters for   years. You can't replace
the feeling of a   hand,   the way; you can get creative
                         back and forth: sketches,
napkins, explications,   stains, photos,   stickers.
          a picture of a can, pull tab opened, revealing a second lid, still
sealed.   "Getting to know me is like,"   it
wasn't true.   the page is all doors and only one ear.
It was his,   I trusted   The   page chooses its
audience.   me for him.   apart   we knitted
            sentences and held ourselves together. We   agree
on the most beautiful part   the
subtle notice   What we sent back and forth: all the
ways to tell a friend *I miss you* just short of saying *I need you in my
life.*   would he know me if I   matter.
I forget   his street, nevermind   We sent
letters, but now we don't.

44

III
We wrote letters   years. You can't replace
                                    the   creative
                              back and forth: sketches,
                  stains,   stickers.

                        to know me is like   it
wasn't   all doors and
            I trusted   The   page
                                                            we knitted
            sentences and held   together.
        the most beautiful part   the
subtle   back and forth:
                        I miss you   *in my*
life.   would   I   matter.
                              nevermind   We sent
letters,   now we don't.

IV
We wrote letters

                                            back and forth:

            now we don't.

Laura Reece Hogan

Persephone at the Turn

On the night of the longest lunar eclipse in five hundred
years, I was the bright skin of the moon

      passing into ruddy
darkness with my handful of torn poppies. The vast
slung undergarment of the abyss bled across
my scuffed countenance

      leaving only a sliver
of my former self. Then I knew how help flies
before us, tips the bowl of new life

      as we move,
decants the courage of ripened fruit. What came before
crosses into after, the shock of a new shape sliding
over the brim. I have focused

      on the rusted shell
when the trajectory is the pale slip of mist, a swelling
trust in the reversal of night. This morning,

      the road eclipsed
in dense marine layer, yellow painted lines
and reflective markers

      emerge in the headlights
just in time, gleaming constellations that spur me
to keep driving over the miles,

      to lean into the silver
thread widening before me, the knot of pomegranate
slowly broken by light, sowing rubies into spring.

Tony Howarth

A Place Not to Call Home

for Auntie Jessie

   down on my hands and knees
attacking the creepy bindweed
   dandelions and sticky willie
which suffocate your headstone

   beyond my understanding
to be told only recently
   you're the daughter of a fling
with an army veteran passing through
   whispered sneers pointed fingers
fostered out by your mum
   her husband when he found out
reluctantly let you live in his home
   let you wash dishes clean the floor
let you serve dinner to his legitimates
   my mum   your half-sister
calling you just a family friend

   before I lived with you I was sent
to shelter with dad's sisters and brother
   they grew anxious sharing wartime rations
passed me along from one to another

   and after I lived with you I was moved again
fostered out to an elderly child-hungry couple
   swanky bedroom with carpet and cushions
tumble-down greenhouse to play in alone

   I've scratched your headstone clean
gathered the weeds into two big piles
   you baked me my favorite biscuits
read me your favorite fairy tales
   plucked the lice from my hair
laughed through your anger
   blamed yourself for sending me to school

47

where they crawled all over my head
    all the time we spent together
dear family friend
    you understood didn't you
how it feels to not belong

Heather Jessen

Sunflowers

If you've been raised by former farm kids,
you already know putting away & cleaning
up is—no exceptions—part of the job. Everything
could kill you—the corn picker, bulls, barbed
wire, tornados, your dad. My uncle once
jumped into the scented invitation
of a haymow & skewered himself straight
through his butt cheek←a pitchfork,
not properly stored. Other fears? Money
for doctors. Fitting in. With English forbidden
at home, subtleties might never be translated
since maybe unconscious & certainly used to draw
the distinction that you were—always—
on the other side of.

Those sunflowers in the ditches—weeds—hacked
down, proof of industry & worth, the scrupulously maintained
margins between your tended field & the road where anyone

could ride by making their own assessment. For decades
my dad hated sunflowers, how readily their merry mocking
faces flourished, creators of backbreaking work
under a relentless sweltering sky. Now he can squint
& acknowledge their bright beckoning. Oh, the irony!,
he laughs. Fancy enough for bouquets; planted—actually
planted!—for the birds! Imagine
what we could have done if we hadn't been chopping
those weeds.

Frederick-Douglass Knowles II

Bury Me in BlackRoseCity

an elegy for Norwich, Connecticut

1.

When I die, bury me in BlackRoseCity,
where Mahan Elementary taught me how to
daydream, sitting at my desk, behind the piano,
Ms. Gilluly's 5th grade class, feigning for McDonalds'
from across the street, chicken McNugget sweet; where Salem
       Turnpike
turned into Great Skate, zooming in & out of electric poles, where
       every
colored complexion caught disco-light fever to roll; where stories
       were told
—too many to capture in my eulogy. Bury me in BlackRoseCity,
       where
Teachers Memorial Junior High field tripped me to Boston and New
York City, strawberry schnapps spilt in the back of the
bus, streaming down the aisle, young, 8th grade
and wild, with Artie, Kevin, Katie, Tara,
Yolanda and Hwa-Chin, where our
infinite bond began, and I found
a handful of lifelong friends.

2.

Bury me in BlackRoseCity,
on the hill between Jane Arms
and Oakwood Knoll, behind Bonanza's
and Zayre's, and let me stare into the Valley of
Thames, where the squirrels will engrave our
names into the coat of their acorns. Bury me in BlackRoseCity,
on the West Side, on the apex of Summit Street, back
when Aunt Nancy's neighborhood was a cultural
crockpot: Jews, Blacks and Browns stirring
the stew, before the recipe eminent domain(ed)
into Dan Jenkins Park. Bury me, at the Block

Party in '83, *The Bridge Is Over* blaring
into the field where the brothas forged
like steel, whenever New London
knuckleheads tried to jump bad,
but headed back down Rt. 32,
mumbling through fat lips
about what they should
of and shouldn't do.

3.

Bury me, in BlackRoseCity
next to: NFA, Mohegan Park,
Hamilton Football Field, East Side,
Laurel Hill, Lake Street, the Red Rabbit,
Sportsmen, Portuguese Club, Johnson Sand Pit,
Bowling Alley birthday parties, Greenville, Taftville
Carnival, Norwich Tech, Young Folk's Shop, Gordon's,
Palace Theater, Norwich Cinema 1 & 2, Barkers, Kings, Ames,
Marcus Plaza, Benny's, Two Legs, Norwichtown Mall Arcade,
Caldor's, Beauland Church, The King Center, Spaulding Pond,
Mohegan Park Zoo, St. Peter & Paul Fair, Uncas, Buckingham,
Veterans, the Sheraton, the Golf Course, Malerba's Farm, Melrose
        Park,
the Dirt Bike Trails, Forward's Pond, East Great Plains Firehouse,
        Delia's,
Vocatura's Bakery, Seafood Etc., the first Kentucky Fried Chicken, the
        PLAV,
VFW, American Legion, Pings, 783, Woolworth's, G. Foxx, the YMCA,
Otis Library, King Wah, Oaktree, Olympic Pizza, nickel night at the
        Village Green, Mohegan
Park Apartments, the Maennerchor, A&P, Bee-Bees, both Friendly's,
        Fairlawns,
Reid & Hughes, Elizabeth (Wood) Street School, the Rec, Masonic
        Temple,
Principal's Mansion, freshman football, Coach Spayden, Coach Mi
        gnault,
Mr. Iovino, Ms. Agrenawich, Mrs. Hendle, Mr. Fields, Mr. Blackstone,
Mr. Snitkin, Mr. Sorello, Mr. Tarka, Mr. Kotraba, Mr. & Mrs. Osko,
my mother, Mrs. Knowles (who took no shit from no student,)

Ms. Fitzgerald, Mrs. Turner, Mrs. Hogan, the City Dump,
Wawecus Hill, Norwich Motel, Charlie's Supermarket,
Scooby's, Radio Shack, Thom McCan's, Genovese,
Uncas on Thames, the State Hospital, Backus,
Crocodiles, Indian Leap, McDonald's,
Friday Night Burger King Parking
Lot Fights, The Falls, Montville
Road, Pizza Hut, TVCCA,
Seaside,"575," before
Wal-Mart was a
vacant lot.

4.

Bury me in BlackRoseCity, in Maplewood Cemetery
next to Gammy, and Eve Montgomery, and Ms. Macy too,
and maybe my roots will seep through the soil for my Saige to see,
how my grandbaby is an extension of legacy, a branch of the Full
          wood Tree,
teach her like LaForest Knowles taught me; how to strap on your
armor and leave
the battlefield bloody. Let me gaze at a Mohegan Sun eclipse; tell the
          city I did it
for them, and I'd do it again, when God gives me a new strategy to
          play the game
again. I did it for my family, yours and mine, and when it's my time,
      tell'em
what I told'em, then tell'em again; that the petals of my city wilt and
renew like a season, leave them with a reason, to garnish the rose
that grew through concrete, Tupacian Philosophy, we've shed
so many tears in this T.H.U.G. L.I.F.E., Dear Mama,
thank you for making me, and raising me, so one
day they bury me, in BlackRoseCity.

Susannah Lawrence

Natural History

I never know when they'll surrender a clue,
      these ice-worn hills—wasp queen's chambered
          nursery, DIY'd out of spittle and wood,

a horned owl's winter barstool, its lurid trash
      below—coughed-up mouse ribs, vole fur,
          teeth—an old cellar hole leaking sorrow.

Some stay encoded, like this wind-growl in the spidery
      reach of sugar maples and red oaks or why you
          once saw a blue crayfish and never again.

Out here lonely mostly a bore, rheumy-eyed—
      same sob stories, same bad breath—no match
          for the sharp intaglio of mink tracks in new snow,

the belch of ice freezing, but today clouds
      hightail south on a run toward spring while I
          dawdle a February field, desperate a little

for a sign living quivers in some egg or chrysalis or
      bee, obedient to sun-time, and in the glum stalks
          of dead asters or goldenrod begins to cha cha.

When three ravens, lobbing calls like kids
      in May dusk, rough the air, jerk evening into play,
          the stubborn delicacy of the trees shoulders

into a slow fade sky though the West goes all in
      theatrical, a yellow-gold I don't have a name for
          but want to be the color of how your chest

will feel against my back tonight, our bodies
      familiar and secret and seasoned, as we
          edge away again from the cold.

Susannah Lawrence

Predicament

Late fall and a blue-gold day on a bluff looking east over Salt Pond Bay
and beyond the Atlantic where tide waters carried Champlain through
the barrier beach along settled shores of the Nausets who lived and
grew old and fed their children on maize and clams and sweet roasted
fish and looked out over the marshy islands channeled and lush with
egrets and herons and ducks, islands now briefly drowned under open
water by a surfeit of tide, a full moon's ordinary work but swollen
by our human needs, our blind want and I'm on the brink of sky and
molten sea blinking in the sun and see now—a dog? stranded 100
yds or so out beyond wind-hustled waves, water licking hungrily at
its belly—no, coyote, all tawny fur and unfathomable eyes, alert and
poised like a dancer ready to leap and staring straight at the bluff,
straight into my eyes, I swear, and asking, no, demanding what is
not in my hands to deliver—rescue—and I will fail, no boat, no oars,
no idea how I would do it anyway, afraid, too, of course, afraid and
inadequate so all I can do is stare back, will her to swim, to strike for
shore, muscles pumping and engorged with blood. Sometimes the
dividing line quivers nearly into vanishing the way islands far away
appear airborne on early fog until the sun burns through to settle them
back into the place. Sometimes it fits like a skin. As if he reads my
mind, the coyote turns away his gaze, slips into current, only his head
visible above blue indifference, strokes landward until lost from view,
swept south deeper into the bay. Perhaps she will clamber out, shake
drowning from her fur the color of forest honey and find her pack—to
chorus the moon in delivery or fellowship, no one to tell them higher
tides are coming, no one who speaks their tongue, even as we listen for
their rowdy songs in our sleep.

Jeffrey Letterly

The Devil of Debt

A hole dug in your yard big
enough for a body or two or a whole
family you try to refill it
with dirt handful by handful
but it takes way too much time and it starts
to rain it doesn't stop raining
the hole beginning to fill up
with rainwater turning it into
a pond you don't want in your backyard
an inground pool you don't want in front
full of murky muddy water but then the sun
comes out and you install a diving board
because that hole isn't going away
it deepens to thirteen feet
and its water so warm go ahead
stick your feet in pull up a plastic
chair make fruity cocktails with umbrellas
invite neighbors and nod heads
as they talk about what a miracle
it is that something that is nothing can grow
how an absence of cashflow
can get bigger and bigger *and the best*
part says Tony *is that you can't*
even see it we all agree
that it can't be real can it
as we look over fences
into each other's yards all of them
with holes a few of them
with an entire moat dug
all around the house
nothing but a narrow path
to get to the front door.

Jeffrey Letterly

Late Night

Cat on a doorstep
waiting to be let in
and a slow snowfall,

the kind that floats
down to the street
then hovers above

the black asphalt. I can't
decide what I like
better—blank

winter or the gush
of spring or
the first sip

of tea in the morning,
almost burning, or
that song by Donna Summer,

the one that was always
on in the background
forty-two years ago,

the one that's easy
to dance to and yet
heartbreaking now

in a way
you can't explain
and would never

tell anyone about.

David Lloyd

Eye of the Storm

This evening, a knotting and tumbling of clouds—
the highest branches trembling, scraps of blue
shrinking. A leaf threads an uncertain path down
and through a tree's airy tangle. There are nights
when I know exactly what to do.
And nights like this, when I simply fall

through my own labyrinth. Does the late fall
cardinal on our feeder see the clouds
blackening, feel the silence? What will he do
when those clouds squeeze the last blue
to nothing and evening becomes night
too soon? He'll hurry home, hunker down

while the world returns to origins: down
and outside, up and inside. He'll fall
with broken wings—it could happen, if night
collapses into detonations of clouds,
the whiplash crack of light, the end of blue.
In this nowhere moment, what can we do

but pray that our wings survive the wind? We do
pray, don't we? faithless on our knees when down
is anywhere, up is elsewhere, blue
is black. That was our state at the fall:
fledglings dumped from the first nest—with clouds
disgorging, saturating the night.

That eye in the storm. Exquisite night
when we know nothing. Doing, not doing,
wings, legs, leaves, branches, earth, clouds
that cannot stop their knotting and tumbling. Down
is up, up is nowhere, the distant fall
is nearly now. The once everywhere, bright blue

of the sky's dome denies blueness.
Now we're leaping into night
without sight of the next instant. The body falls
while the mind's wings keep beating. Do
what? you ask. What? Here's what: Go down,
into the circus of storm, the within of clouds,

empty branches where blue will never do,
the night bodies, the tumbling, clouded down.
We fall. We dive. We dive into clouds.

David Lloyd

What the Snake Said

That man, you would think, has it all: A god
to believe in. Always-ripe fruit. A woman
made of rib. An empty sky above:
no moon, no stars, so he won't feel penned in
by the unseen limits of paradise—
crowded with beasts, fish, fowl. And a snake

with legs and a quick, forked tongue—a snake
with charm, on a first name basis with god.
But this snake has questions: "Is paradise
perfect enough?" he asks the man. "Or woman
woman enough? Sky real enough? In-
sects resilient enough? What shapes lie above

our words? Do we truly want to breathe and love
without shame? Am I in fact a snake,
or a god dethroned, deveined, shrink-wrapped in
snakeskin by a taller god? Is our god
not transcendent but a man who proved man
enough to take a bite out of paradise,

so he might know more than the word "paradise"—
know this very place, below sky yet above
earth? Listen: I know what's to come: woman
and man eat, touch, and die; the doubting snake
writhes on the earth, legless, despised; and god
restricts paradise to the cherubim

and himself." The snake gulped some air in-
to his air sac. "You must roll the dice,"
he told the man and woman. "Forget your god's
forbidden name. Take a look below, above.
Wonder if every sun-bathing snake
is a god wrapped up, and every woman

a god unwrapped, and every naked man
the same. Pluck the fruit. Lift it. Sink in
your teeth. Ignore the worm. Then forgive the snake
his words. Forgive yourselves. For paradise
has a feel if you take off the gloves.
And though I'll never walk again, and God

will never love a snake, I hope that woman
and man might see me, and themselves, in time, in
this lost paradise, below and above."

Melissa McKinstry

Ode to the Beet

From a wrinkled seed: the round eye of the storm,
the funnel cloud–how it sweeps robes
of verdant leaves across the garden bed and sky.
In just-spring it offers itself,
and we rinse the coppery silt
in the sink, peel each globe. The satisfaction
of the sharp knife, the intelligent smell–
liquor and petrichor. Next, the shudder
of foil over the sheet pan,
the glisten of olive oil and salt,
the perfume of thyme.
How we sip a simple merlot, inhale
the mercy of roasting, the scent
of everything the beet learned
underground. How our fingers twine,
jewel stained, longing,
as we spin a slow kitchen dance
and rain silvers the windows.
Oh, winter vegetable devoured by Aphrodite
to amplify her charms. Graffitied
on the walls of *lupanares* in Pompeii,
the erotic portraits of Bull's Blood
and Ruby Queen survived
even the rush of Vesuvius.
Who hasn't had an hour
when burrowing in the earth
seemed perfectly reasonable?
How to be absent even to birdsong,
to listen instead to another root
reaching. How taking in the earth
through each filament must be.

Melissa McKinstry

The Present Participle Gives Instructions on the Continuous Tense

For months I've been waking at 3:33,
the moment I watched my father dying
in a hospital room filling with shadows.

The owls, the foghorn,
and the train keep moaning.
Sometimes a thin siren starts calling from a distance,
a red thread raveling the lapel of night.

Sometimes Venus and the waxing moon
are traveling companions in the south-facing window
singing the sound of silence like Simon and Garfunkel.

There's always a silken hunger in dawn's slip of light
shining on the hardwood, climbing the bookshelves.
I keep drinking tea. The cat keeps leaping
onto the desk, looking me in the eye,
then resting her chin on *Walden*, purring.

I keep walking into these cold mornings,
passing a child kicking along on a scooter,
an old man wearing a watch cap
and wool gloves.

Feel how soft this is, Melissa,
my father would say, brushing my hand
against his new chamois shirt.
Feel how warm.

Rennie McQuilkin

Migrations

It is all different now: war rages in the East
and has invaded our hearts and heads.
Nothing seems real but civilians slaughtered,
their homes' rubble littered with torn shoes,
spines of books, parts of stuffed animals
and their owners.

The living attempting escape by safe corridors
during times of truce are shot down.
Refugees bearing little but loss clog the roads
under dark clouds of acrid smoke.

This should be a joyful time. Spring is coming
and the Great Migration of amphibians
has started—salamander, wood frog and
Hyla crucifer bearing a dark cross.
I want not to think of the hazards they face:
rushing traffic raging on roads they must cross
and predators waiting along their corridors
leading to rare havens in wetlands.

I cheer for them but this year am too aware
of the terrible odds. I pray for them,
for all migrants and refugees.

Dan Murphy

Pall Bearing

A pack of cigarettes. A languorous
air. Pair of spit-shined shoes. A plain, black suit.
Four fingers' worth of whiskey. Handkerchiefs.
A steady arm, unyielding grip. A new
grey cap I fix and nod. The sod beneath
my damp, cold feet: a softness shouldering
this empty heft. Today there is this grief
that has no bottom. Tolling bell, it rings
with ritual. There's keening, wan and loud.
And music in the ceiling. When we roll
your body down the pews, I listen how
they hymn. Imagine breath again: white pall
of winter lifted, every thought a thread,
your soul a linen snapping in the wind.

Meryl Natchez

Meditation on War

*The difference between dreaming of a reordered world and dreaming
of reordering it oneself as one sees fit is a profound and fatal one...*
— Vladimir Nabokov

1

Stone, club, the Masai's cow-hide shields,
sword craft of Japan, catapult,
fortress and siege engine, gunpowder,
the caterpillar treads of the tank,
missiles and missile defense,
hydrogen, nitrogen, neutron, drone.
What if we need it?

What if we need it
the way forests need fire?
Seeds release in the heat,
the ground charred
clear for them.

2

The man in shirtsleeves and tie
paces hot asphalt,
gestures and shouts,
no phone in sight:
If I get hold of you, I'll fuck you...
You want to play your frigging games?
I'll play...

War starts in the heart,
in the attachment
the Buddhists warn us about,
the same monks who touched the match
to their own doused robes
turning their flesh into torches.

3

In a slow unfolding of white, an egret arcs up
over the cars, the rust and mud of the flats,
its map different from ours,
though bound by the laws of this earth,
the tides that soak the black ooze to silver—
this transient, city-rimmed sky mirror.

Peter O'Donovan

The Radiance

> *Due to flawed calculations, the average color of the universe*
> *was originally thought to be turquoise.*
> *— "Cosmic Latte," Wikipedia.*

Instead we're bathed in temperate beige,
the frothy micro foam of Cosmic Latte.
A tame color, timidly whipped and poured
too quick, suggestive of office hallways
or the soft clothes of the upwardly mobile.
A color calculated to be average,
the sum of something uncountable,
some spectral estimation of radiance,
of the faint flares of hermetic galaxies.
Still, it's a better name than Cosmic Cream,
and even the Greeks claimed the Milky Way
was Hera's breast milk sprayed across the pitch
when a teething Hercules took a nip.
Precedent has been set, or rather misted
upon that dark matter, that espresso void
mostly cloaked, its surface swirling with stars:
those in their blue youth with feverish heat,
the stolid middle-aged giving off gold,
or elderly reds, late phase but still blazing,
all blended together in spiral systems,
in clusters of galaxies, with light enough
to draw us up into the magnitude
of all that is beyond, all that elsewhere
slowly flowing by in the night, a flood
of billions of billions of other suns
suffusing us with their luminous hue.

Kurt Olsson

Livelihoods

You carry a piece of the cross with you,
the true cross, the cross he died on, the cross
a man fashioned, the cross measured and sawed,
chiseled and fitted, the man understanding
the provenance of wood, how to work it,
what a span of wood can and cannot bear,
picturing what he was making but not
for whom, just as another might not know
for whom a hammer or lamb's shoulder was intended.
A man who viewed his making as a way
to earn a livelihood, the means for keeping alive,
of putting food on the table. If shavings fell
from his brow, if he pulled a splinter from a callused
thumb and it bled a little, the sawdust and blood
mixing with what was on his plate didn't alter
the taste of what he ate. Didn't make him think
of what he had or had not done that day.

S.E. Page

Tiny Cakes

I can't stop buying tiny cakes online:
Miniature Swarovksi confections in crystal,
sumptuous desserts small enough to fit
superbly as a cherry in the palm of my hand.
I buy four in a few hours and trigger a fraud alert
on my credit card, and I wonder if maybe—
I'm faking me.

I was supposed to be going all Marie Kondo
on my house, gutting it of sparkless things.
At first, I minimized with ruthless efficiency,
ditching bags of books my mother once read me,
and boxes of her dolls with bright glass eyes
I always meant to save for
my future littles.
But there will be
none of that
now—

What am I to do with this body of years
already stripped down of hopes?
My flesh betrays me
in ways I will never forgive,
scarring all my moments
with chronic breakdowns
I still don't understand.
I must live afraid of food,
and what will happen in bathrooms,
if just daring to walk outside might
trigger another piece of me
to go wrong.

Maybe that's why I suddenly hunger for tiny cakes—
shiny slices of little perfections not for eating,
only the anticipation of imaginary flavors,
some future happiness that will never dim

and disappoint me as long as I dust it.
Let me go all Marie Antoinette!
Give me CAKE, such bright delights—
I will set each of these wishful treats
out on a shelf, sweet bitsy dreams,
and kindle myself new sparks
of timed joy just for
a tiny today.

Ryan Parker

"I'm Black like that."

I'm going to allow myself to be pushed from the echoes of the earth
Self-induced reparations for all I am worth
And this pull—
With my own hands
Shedding the snakeskin
Of false narratives the script dictated
And orchestrated
By Conditions outside of my own
But I OWN me
My body my home
And I am evicting every trauma-filled tenet
Every stereotype threat
Holding myself
My own body in my own arms
Remembering the sacredness of this home
Remembering my ancestors prayed me into existence
Filling my body with beautiful dark allowing the stars my spirit is
made of
To ignite with delicious delight
But I am *NOT* star
I am *WORLD.*
Sacred land
Oceans and all
World-penning poem
Holding myself and refusing to let go
Magic of me—
Oh magic of me!
BEAUTIFUL BLACK BODY!
Trauma is NOT your native language
Keep being Black like seeds
Like the richest soil for them to enter
For them to bloom—
Black like calla lily—
Like contrast against the moon—
Like wide peppered spots on ladybug backs
Black like sweet licorice

Be Black like that!
Like an opening to somewhere—
Black infinite space to something
Black like eyes shut clamshell tight—relaxed
Black like sun-lit wings of crows
Indigo rose tomato Black
Poem ink on page…
BLACK!

Marge Piercy

Gardening in the Woods

We live in the end of a development
where it peters out into woods.
We garden, but not in the suburban
way. Three vegetable gardens

take priority and feed us all year
after we freeze, can and dry.
Neighbors whose house is invisible
behind trees hire locals to clear,

plant, weed—nothing to harvest.
They call our house The Jungle.
Roses clamber over the gazebo.
Our flowers are mostly food

for pollinators except for peonies
that fill a raised bed and roses
planted over our cats who died.
Three acres left natural for those

who lived here before us and will
persist after we've gone to earth.
No, it isn't neat. Black currants
run rampant. Sugar maples,

white firs, weeping beech, sour
cherry, pears half a century old.
This land is like us: organic,
fecund, original, and messy wild.

Carol Potter

a boundless repetition of small events

You could be the body that breaks things.
The one who walks on the cold frame

in the drying yard. You could be the one
who held the clothesline and thought she could

walk above the small heads of lettuce
across a pane of glass. You could be that light child.

The magic girl. You could be the one who thought
the glass was magic. The sneakers on your feet

magic. Of course it breaks. You could be
that girl crashing through. You could be

the one who came screaming out of that yard
bleeding. You could be the one marked. The skin

broken. The cold frame broken. The clothes
line broken. Glass shards in your hands.

Geri Radacsi

Susie Hot Rod

That red Corvette blams,
      revs a V-8 blast,
every piston purred.
Amplified static from the past: 1955,
      her first drag race. No helmet,
no seat belts, not even a tool brought along—but
      her blonde hair braided tightly.
      She downshifts to third and floors the gas,
skirts sideways, corrects, pulls out to pass.

      Classy-cool, but reckless, her husband foresees:
Crash. Explosion. Flames.
      Tuned to revs he's built in that engine,
he'd turned cars rad, three one-barrel carbs and three manifolds
ready to rip up the Roadrunners. And Torinos.

      Four on the floor to lay rubber in every gear
until bolder and bolder the roar,
      Susie leaves
men behind. The field is lost, exhaust.

Exhilaration. She feels complete
      while her man worried, carried wrenches clanging,
his knuckles nicked by drops of blood.
Parts of their lives
      are pieced into each other,
painstaking precision to hit all specs.

Their engine barks, bites as it gulps
      its mixtures and screams, the louder, the better.
Otherwise a quiet couple,
whose hot rods found each other,
their marriage, a controlled
      explosion—Waaaaaaaww!
Wedding day cans
      strung on their back bumper bang

out a charivari—
enliven the main drag.

Time, full-throttle, blurs and weaves.
        Susie wears white wonderfully woven hair,
skids into an unreal world of forgetting
as if she's only been driving through.

James Ragan

Exorcising the Lane

Each autumn when I walk the dirt barefoot
and memorize the lane's long language
in the dead breath of leaves,
I hear the stone's hard breathing
beneath the late snow of October,
the sun-grunt in the moss shoal of its stomach,
the fast fall of dust feeding my brain,
remembering how I'd ride the sky to pasture
high on the cow's peak in March,
my world-war brother limping,
shank to thighs in mud bottling his feet.
I still hear the gurgling ground-swallow
of his shoe leavings, the lost believings
he held incarnate like fate
or scars etched into his wounded leg.
In my mind his gone life stokes the dust
of memory into the lane's earth birthing
of his cursing cries. My mother heard
the lane's death-breath across the rug
she'd broom-beat in the winds of June,
in nest seeds threshed from the rain spout,
in soot from the scope of my outdoor cup.
Each spring I'd await her cleansing
of the soil from my tongue. Always
the lane coursing its breath to my throat,
and always my mother beating it back,
dust-swollen, standing her own dark ground.

Lindsay Rockwell

Dear Unknown,

Yesterday the sky went blank.
The soft-spoken woman was climbing.
Out of her car. Into the tall grass then.
Got down on her knees. She seemed. One time
too many human. She held her hand up. Palm pushing
north into the wind. Suddenly.
Sound was extinguished.
There was air. And the inside
of nothing.
I don't think I'll ever forget her.
I've been thinking about you since.
Your garden feels. Aimless
this spring. The thickets are amok with voiceless
bullfrogs. Unsettling. Tonight
under the worm moon. I will.
Plant my weight. On the edge of the pond. Hope
for a faint croak to slip through dark's seam.
Did I mention. I'm scared.
Because it feels. Like I'm stepping
into a pile of dreams. Some perversion.
Or infection. Translated into a mutant
that fits my fears just right.
Anyhow. I'm sorry.
Bothering you with all this.
The water's run
out. The sound's turned
off. The sky's gone
blank. And the babies.
I mean the children. They've given up.
Walking. I hope I haven't scared you off.
I remember. Last time we lay
in the forest darkness fell. Like an overdue prayer.
As we drifted off to sleep. I confessed. My obsession
with silence.
Anyhow. The world
has still not ended.

The children won't walk but I can tell they're listening. Frozen
in the sun.
Can't wait to see you.
One of these days.
Love,
L

Edwin Romond

Kindness

for Philip Levine (1928-2015)

There was just one seat left
in the hotel van bringing us
back to the Poetry Festival
and I was nervous when you,
a nationally known poet,
took that seat next to me,
an un-nationally known poet
hired, not to read my poems,
but to help with parking cars.
What could you and I talk about
for the 15 minute ride? But
you grinned when you sat down,
asked my name and when
I said I was a high school teacher
you joked, "So, Ed, what's it like
teaching teenagers these days?"
and words between us flowed easily
till suddenly the van braked
in front of police lights flashing red
around a deer just hit by a car,
alive but belly-whopping in agony
in the middle of the highway.
The squad car turned sideways
to block our view then a loud
gun shot that jolted me back
in my seat. "You okay, Ed?"
you asked and put your hand
upon my arm, one man
caring about another's pain,
the first truth of being alive.

Rikki Santer

How to Outwit Oblivion

> *after Artemisia (2020 catalogue from The National Gallery in London)*
> *and for painter Artemisia Gentileschi (1593-1653)*

We reread across centuries to retrieve you,
your canvases—elastic moments like, yet like

no other Baroque. Seconds split open,
rhythms of your tread. By stuttering

candlelight you are lungs of your house.
Your zaftig women whispering *God*

Oh God, their horror / their ligaments
of desire look right through us.

The Russian dolls of your badger-hair
brush—women within women, echoed

currency of your face, grammar of their manly
hands. You, eager protégé who took bites of

raw sunrise, a caged goldfinch in your father's
bottega. Hungry eyes, you learned to think with

your body, muscle of your lens, beetroot on your lips,
dark undercoat and gentileschi golds for suffering

heroines. Time slips. Rape trial in tabloid moon shadow.
Dissertations, movies, novels torque your story, wedge

you into what's illustrative. You, royal artist for parceled
flesh tones and calibrated scenes. You, maestra who finds

purchase again and again. Seemed seams of history
intervene, and you standing on top of the stars,

your signature in Clio's open book,
your ear-finger wagging.

Maria Sassi

Cat on a Winter Beach

At first star she comes out over the causeway
from behind Fitzgerald's mansion. Most nights
she rubs against the pilings,
barnacles of sea towns where cat's hair strays.

Tonight she curves her small spine away from the wind,
finds the cave the old tarp made and curls under.
She seems to be listening to the music
of the off-hinged door to the rickety cabaña—

slam-shut-open...slam-shut-open.

The sound would remind her of that underbeat of drum
come summer over the water from jazz pavilions.
Her first lap of champagne—silver saucer—
fizz tipping her cap-pink tongue.

Hot moons! The beginning of July!

She snakes in deeper and tightens against the cold.
Keeping one eye out to the sky, she must wonder
why she comes here when she can be warm
in the watchman's shed, all warning bells
of the sea buried in her dreaming head.

Out here, on this pier, she must face the winter—
hope for the moon's thin lift of light,
for a wind shift to southerly,
an opening of green-celled seasons in her blood,
entering the locks and pump of the chamber—

slam-shut-open...slam-shut-open.

The sweet sprung rhythms in her cat-bone cage
beat in her veins of a warming coast,
of a green sea leaving salt in her blood,

a moonrise spreading light wide as holy summer.

The beach turns on its private axis
under the blazing Southern Cross,
the wind's long fall...
comes a music she knows she knows,
a sounding hum, coming from light—

slam-shut-open...open...open

James Scruton

Bucket List

As the conversation turns to Matterhorn
and Machu Picchu, to sky-dives
and snorkeling among sea turtles,
I find myself considering instead
the bucket, wondering

if it's a grey tin pail
like the ones we used to husk corn into
on my in-laws' farm, the kind
of bucket we can imagine someday kicking
with a clattering fanfare all our own.

Maybe a plastic bucket at the beach,
saltwater streaming out through holes
the way time does through our sandy fingers,

or else an old wooden bucket,
a few slats cracked but held in place
by a couple of thin iron ribs,
a real antique by now
and just for show perhaps,
a pot for flowers on the porch,
for an umbrella or pair of muddy shoes
beside the door, for whatever we may need
in our not-too-distant future.

James Scruton

Other Muses

O for a Muse of fire…
(Henry V)

Passé, perhaps, a Muse of air,
the original *vent*
of our invention,
heavenly *-spire* breathing
into us out of the blue.

But why not a Muse of water,
spring rain against the windows
unstrain'd as any quality
of Portia's mercy,
each pond and puddle later
full of sky? Let me dip
my pen into Hamlet's sea
of troubles, let me read
the good Duke's books
in all those running brooks.

Even a Muse of earth
would do, loamy ink
across my page, gravelly voice
in my ear. Let me furrow
and trench, be topsoiled,
gritty. O Muse, let me dig
to the bottom of things.

Vivian Shipley

Beethoven's *Missa Solemnis*

Ice coats everything, frozen again this morning
into a glossy crust, scarred and scarred
again, by the dogs' crossing. I can picture Lucifer

in *Canto XXXIV* of Dante's *Inferno*, imprisoned
not in a fiery pit but in the remorseless dead center
of a lake of unyielding ice, the final 9th circle

in hell for those who betrayed their family,
committed treachery against those with special ties.
I'm sinking in shame over words shouted

at my husband who like Beethoven is almost deaf.
Snow persists like anger built month by month
grinding pills, funneling carton after carton

of liquid food through my husband's stomach tube.
To right myself, I read Beethoven's words
inscribed in *Missa Solemnis* to Archduke Rudolf

of Austria: *From the heart: may it reach the heart.*
His music may make my world bearable for a while.
It's probably fifty-three minutes before I hear what

must have made it hard for Leonard Bernstein
to breathe while conducting the mass. In *Sanctus*,
the prelude of meditative strings with support

from flutes ushers in a radiant violin solo
in pure G major at its highest range, entering like
a dove from heaven representing the Holy Spirit

descending to earth, *Him who comes in the name
of the Lord.* I gain solace from God's holiness
but in the final *Agnus Dei*, I hear what I am seeking,

that an appeal for outer and inner peace is far
from fulfilment, far from menacing sounds of war,
trumpets and timpani drum rolling almost to an end.

Still, I'll hum Beethoven's *Blessed is he who
cometh in the name of the Lord*; it might lead me
to a riff, a song, even to a prayer, even to patience.

Tara Skurtu

Mirror Method

my mother
and I aim for the invisible spot
I've gotten this far
two tables away
my mother becomes a mirror
a pool stick away
aim here, she says
I haven't gotten that far in life yet
the cue ball lands
you're supposed to know where
all the best players know

all the best players know
you're supposed to know where
the cue ball lands
I haven't gotten that far in life yet
aim here, she says
a pool stick away
my mother becomes a mirror
two tables away
I've gotten this far
and I aim for the invisible spot
my mother

John L. Stanizzi

Journeys

A journey is a person in itself; no two are alike.
—John Steinbeck, Travels with Charley: In Search of America

Show me where to begin this morning,
how to sit with the overcast dawn
and consider what has been said
and what will be said
waiting patiently for the rain.

Soon the birds will make their voyage.
This morning's silent valley reminds us of that.
And the leaves will burn their smokeless burn,
leaving a landscape of naked bones,
each one distinct, each one with story...

—here there was a nest,
—there a fledgling wobbled,
—and the branches with the gentle arch
are the ones that bent for the wind,
moved aside to let it pass;

—the fallen branches,
—the ones face down on their bellies...
those are the ones crawling
ever so slowly
back to where they started

Samn Stockwell

Piecework

I will tell you exactly what happened
without fabrication. The owner
perched the iguana on my shoulder,
stuffed her toddler in my other arm
and took off in her red car.

I was making my first visit to her.
I was pacing in the driveway
when she returned to take possession—

a wonderful phrase, inadequate
for the reality of ownership.
You have something: a child, a disease,
a coin collection and it's yours to carry—

unless someone drops by
to aid in lifting you above the plateau
you are stalking in a mild fever.

She, wrapped in the burs
at the edge of her vision,
put her child down
on a counter at the market.
He reappeared in sales bins,
drugstores, the homes of distant relatives.

When winter turned all the water to glass,
he skated back to her.

John Struloeff

The Dream

Albert Einstein, 1939

That night he had a dream,
something beyond a nightmare.
He'd had only one other like it
after his father died, that
made him weep, left him shaken
for days. It burned his psyche,
a flash of brilliant, terrifying
light that would vaporize flesh
and obliterate bone. The light
came from a star on earth,
something he could hardly
imagine. All would be beyond
shadows. All would look into
the heated eye of a god
he had only begun to see.

John Surowiecki

The Isthmus of Children from Broken Homes

The ocean on the right is gray and angry and
so is the one on the left.
They aren't encouraged to touch and there's
no way to connect them. The continent in front
claims the future, the one behind the past. Both have
cobalt lakes and up—
flowing rivers and trees
that cough up clouds.

Footprints in the sand are like dents in a steel drum.
The tide swallows them the way time swallows music.
Anemometers made
from paper cups and popsicle sticks catch the wind
blowing in from all directions all at once. The night is a
suburb of thunder and rain,
promising sleep
but not allowing it.

Matthew Thorburn

In Translation

The red-tailed hawks wheeling overhead
as Preston and I walk home turn out
to be turkey vultures. Chuck Wilkens
taught us to notice the slight V of their wings
on one of our Sunday hikes in the grasslands
near Griggstown, his tired voice muffled
by a blue mask and the six feet we kept
between us all afternoon. I woke up

to read it in an email: Chuck passed away
last night. Now my young son raises his fist,
shouts in Mandarin, "Go away, vultures!
You can't eat us. We're not dying today!"
He translates for me, glancing back
as he walks ahead. What else can I do,
stumbling after him in this cold
brown field, but shake my fist too?

Matthew Thorburn

Ladybug

Or lady*bird*. I remember that's another name when I spot the speckled half-globe of its candy-red shell as I'm getting ready for bed. Little button circling the lip of the sink. At least I think it is. They go so slowly. And I'm so *something*—bemused? pleased? — that I say this out loud: *Honey, I'll just carry you back outside.* She creeps closer to the faucet. Or *he* does—how can you tell? I'd never swat a ladybug. Lillian says even to find a dead one is bad luck. My toothbrushing on hold, I hold out a magazine reply card for it to step onto—*Come on, now*—then deposit the ladybug in my hand. It's tiny, weightless; its steps along my palm I can't feel. Gently I cup one hand over the other, a gesture between praise and prayer. Then together we step out the door, into the dark.

Carol Was

For the Callery Pear, Survivor Tree

When the towers fell, steel melted
and the ground shook your roots, tore
them apart. Shredded paper fluttered
from the sky. Metal debris on fire
gouged limbs and trunk, branded you
like a steer with a hot iron. Something
forced one branch to call for rescue
using your only voice, fresh leaves.
Unnatural time to bloom in October.
Found barely alive, you were the last
living thing pulled from that horror.
Nine years to nurse wounds, cultivate
new roots. You made it back, gnarled
arms scarred, your runes telling
the carnage. We read your skin,
bark Braille. Your trauma line mimics
the K-Pg Boundary. You thrive
replanted at Ground Zero. A sign
of hope, your seedlings, sent
as gifts, grow around the world.

Pamela Wax

The Little Prince Said It First

What is essential is invisible to the eye —
knowing this to be true, troubled
by what I saw straight-on
and sideways in my periphery,
I set my eyes on building heaven
on earth, as naive, some thought,

as that golden-curled space
traveler with his signature scarf.
By then I had words for *calling*
and *sacred*, for *glory* and *grace*,
and for the animal spirit galloping
in me, its invitation to wrangle

clouds into patterns of meaning,
ride dolphins bareback into town,
defender of children and other living
things, and to lie belly-up
like a cat, exposed, because students
want to see how the rabbi ties her shoes.

I trained to spelunk in caves
of the heart, certain of the patience
of bulbs below ground. I sniffed hard-
to-reach blessings in crevices
of human grief, even when miles
and months away, like a polar bear

on the scent of a seal three feet
under ice. By then I knew synesthesia
was a paradox of spiritual
wholeness, like John Locke's
blind man who smelled the color
scarlet when he heard a trumpet blast.

I, too, touch and taste red when the alarm
rouses me to the world ablaze,
the Garden distant. That's when I miss
my mother and think of the rose
alone in the bell jar, the one
we're all called to raise.

Scott Wiggerman

Pause

with a nod to Rebecca Dunham's "This Is a Letter"

This is a moon for a January so cold
the roots of Ponderosa pines shiver.
A moon whose light is distant and fading
like the last flickers of a galaxy long extinguished.
A moon whose best friend is a headstone.

This is a moon for the hungry with gravel in their mouths,
for the thirsty with water deep
out of reach in the bowels of the earth,
for the final phone call, the last email,
          the terrible alone.

This is a moon that doesn't rise,
or if it does, never shows more than
a clipped fingernail of its yellowed self.
This is a moon for the numb,
for arms that can't feel and legs that won't move.
A moon for a time when there is
no tide, no warnings, no new moon.

This is a moon for the miserable
whose fingers grasp ever-shifting grains.
This is a desert moon too long on hold,
an orphan huddling for a sliver of warmth.

Charles Wilkinson

From All Sides

—at you from all sides
& it's not just that it knows
            when to alter the angle
  or how to come
            cutting under a canopy
riding with the strut of winds
& springing white sticks from a path—
            the swanking rain
tricked out in all the conceits of water
  —it's what rises from the mud,
  laughing in runnels
   the burst pipes' music of flow
running showy in the gutters
it's how the gale picks up a flood
    & throws it
            over hedges
flattening furrows to a gleam of fields
    it's the breaking of the banks
the river's throat swallowing earthy assets

the innocence of rain is over
what once gave comfort
to the child in a bed beneath
the skylight is the pity of storms persisting:
a bridge crumpled by a river's paw
the roads transformed to streams
a flood demanding an open door
& each wet day the descent of a city
    the levels ascend
      the cliffs shiver to scree
    shrinking land's end
   to the aims of erosion
            till towns
            are taken
            out to sea—

Charles Wilkinson

Hidden at the Edge of a Field

morning waves its hands, palms open, as if innocent.
    already the light cuts & plays, double-dealing.
a message, hidden in cloud, is sealed. landscape
    feigns faith in itself: the wood's frankly a wood;
yet this leafless tree here, isn't its trunk hollow?
    at half past three a church's shadow conceals
the card of darkness in its sleeve; a meadow
    in the long afternoon mislays its flowers,
    & in the lake the missing child lies, waiting
for a drought to drain, so death can be revealed

the evening's uncertain gold trips over the earth
    where a wheat field shone, inferring treasure below.
now men come slow-walking for metal, detecting,
    bowed as if talking to soil, listening for sounds,
summoned up from the sleep of centuries: trove
    undercover in the ground – & the dusk thickens,
as they miss by metres, the hoard: the silver torque,
    a cache of coins, the boss of a vanished shield,
the tip of a spear, a buckle & brooch found near
    the bier of a nameless king, his tongue lost,
    his thoughts deep sunk for a thousand years.

Christie Max Williams

Stars for Susan

Where are you, friend? I need your voice, your face.
I long to watch you listening to me,
to know myself a glowing commonplace
in your affection, to feel you simply be.
O meet me at the usual café,
yes, the one where I am always late,
where the wine makes no demands on what we say,
where we can be a night to celebrate.
At the same quiet table sit the ghosts
of our best selves, waiting to be moved
to laughter—or is it tears? For them let's toast
the luck and mystery of being loved.
Later, passing shuttered shops and bars,
suppose we stop, look up—there might be stars!

Avery Yoder-Wells

Maquette

Nothing is certain but Death and the milkman.
They are both partial to the early morning.
Their van drives endlessly around dark roads,
spilling front walks with embryo yellow.

The milkman does not knock—
they could never be mistaken for strangers.
He rattles bottles like rare pennies
and arranges groups of four on the porch.
Like a cow's stomachs, Death says

and is informed cows have a single stomach
in four parts. They are only hungry once.
The milkman feeds mouths methodically.
His hands are chilled but never sour.

Death prefers threes. When a dog bristles
to protect his residents, Death strokes his head
forward, backward, and from teeth to eye.
His fingers are cold as coin collectors,
emptying each mouth that runs too full.

Death knocks as they leave, just for courtesy.
Like a salesman, his partner says. The mortician
and the moratorium. One peddles starvation
so the other can deliver brief reprieve.

Each could be either. Both are natural discomforts,
and houses hunger every morning of their lives.
So Death and the milkman drive, gently,
warming fingers between the other's hands.

CONNECTICUT POETRY SOCIETY
PRIZE WINNERS

Experimental Poetry Contest, 2021
Judge: Richard Deming

Winner
makalani bandele
"Afropessimism 101: Quiz on System of Weights Used (1619-Present)"

About the Judge: Senior Lecturer in English and Director of Creative Writing at Yale University, Richard Deming is a poet, art critic, and theorist whose work explores the intersections of poetry, philosophy, and visual culture. His poetry collection *Let's Not Call It Consequence*, received the Norma Farber Award from the Poetry Society of America.

makalani bandele

Winner, Experimental Poetry Contest, 2021

"Afropessimism 101: Quiz on System of Weights Used (1619-Present)"

To view the winning poem from the 2021 Experimental Poetry Contest, visit the link below and scroll down a little on the web page. https://ctpoetry.net/experimental-poetry.html

To hear the poem, scan the QR code below.

Connecticut Poetry Award, 2021
Judge: Rennie McQuilkin

1st Prize
Richard Levine
"Is!"

2nd Prize
Taylor Lynn Copeland
"Necessary Solitude"

3rd Prize
Ellen Hirning Schmidt
"Saving Salamanders"

About the Judge: Rennie McQuilkin, who has served as Connecticut's Poet Laureate, is the author of numerous poetry collections, several of which have won major awards. He co-founded and for years directed the Sunken Garden Poetry Festival at Hill-Stead Museum in Farmington, Connecticut. He runs an independent poetry press, Antrim House Books. McQuilkin is the recipient of the Connecticut Center for the Book's Lifetime Achievement Award.

Richard Levine

First Prize, Connecticut Poetry Award, 2021

Is!

in memoriam, Joe Hayman (1938-2017)

I had gone to take the bare trees of my thoughts to walk
in the park, seeking consolation in goose honks, coot dives,
the lily-white of swans beneath the ominous
red-tailed glide of a hawk, and the small talk of a sidewalk
bush, alive with dozens of chirping sparrows.
Dozens. Chirping. For today, I was bound to bear
my heart like sad hands hiding in shallow pockets.

Since the news, grief has collected and disquieted
memories tangled like fish lines, sticky, blood-barbed hooks,
sinkers, snares, bobbers and bones,
all thrown in and cast to rattle a racket in a gray pail,
where the stink's cooked in and as sharply pronounced
as the cacophonous, sad-handed carrying of it.

To no avail, I *am* parading in grave-muddy boots,
as if passing like a clarion every hearth where our names
are known and called *is* helpful—Am! Are! Is!
Damned present tense!
Dear friends, our superlatives are but a palliative ruse,
for we have gathered today to past tense our friend's every verb,
pull out each one like a dead fish from a bucket.

What, but an inevitable occupation.
Tis true, tis pity; tis pity, tis true.

But come, cast each in his chowder pot and gather edible nouns—
fish heads first, then turnips and beans, parsnips and greens,
coriander and fenugreek, for a stew he'd simmer all day,
to shut winter's windows and doors against itself,
because gray is a lonely ache.
Is! Again!
Here! give a stir, as he did, humming arias and songs
over the stewing pot, maybe *En Tarbena Quando Sumus*

or *Lydia the Tattooed Lady*. And open plenty of wine bottles
for the long nights and the cold heave.

And come, call on every creature to sing
for a dear friend, a sweet choir-voice, which first rose
in the building of ricks under barn-lofts and weathervane-skies.
And that boy, that hay-man boy who would one day want to feed
and sing for everyone he knew—for he knew how we were
all always so hungry and what for—
that fine fellow, ... my dear friend, ... is dead; is no more is.

Listen, as I was telling you,
this morning, as I wandered the park,
my bare tree thoughts encaged a hawk
not twenty feet above where I stood.
In its thrall, I watched the graceful swivel
of its head and eyes, its bullet-body
as still and hard as its raptor-beak.
But its feathered majesty could not fool me,
not today; I know what its swift,
hollow-boned villainy is here to undo.
Is! Is!

Taylor Lynn Copeland

Second Prize, Connecticut Poetry Award, 2021

Necessary Solitude

Ask me *what does peace feel like*, & I will remember
the scent of woodsmoke & the soft hush of late August
as I stepped out of my car & into that mild afternoon
in the Catskills. There was the cabin, my tiny home
away from home. I was alone, & it was quiet.

Ask me *why didn't you check your phone*, & I will think
of how the wide picture window framed
the lush summer forest as I lay in bed & rested
for the first time all year, bare legs cool
under a rumpled white duvet, the kiss
of the morning sunlight kinder than any alarm clock.

Ask me *why did you go by yourself*, & I will tell you
about the way dusk braided itself gently through
the trees; the taste of salt on my fingers
as I ate an entire batch of popcorn by the campfire; how
I laid out a blanket on the picnic table as the flames burned low
& let my gaze wander among the stars.

Ask me *why was this the highlight of your year*, & I will ask
if you've ever stopped to stand beneath a waterfall
while out hiking in the woods, or if, amid months
of chaos & conflict, it's so strange to cling to the moments
when you feel at ease. I will ask: when did you last give yourself
the gift of peace? when was the last time you found joy
in the necessary solitude of your soul?

Ellen Hirning Schmidt

Third Prize, Connecticut Poetry Award, 2021

Saving Salamanders

A red eft salamander wriggles across our road as
together my neighbor and I walk six feet apart.
"It's all going to hell in a handbasket," she says as I
lean down, reach my thumb and forefinger
around the soft orange body,
long and flexible like a young string bean,
so supple, so squashy
"We'll not survive it," she adds.
I place the newt near the watery ditch on the side of the road
where she seemed to be heading.
"No income. No food. No health care."
I see another tiny orange body, carry her across to the
other side, where she seems to be journeying
"No infrastructure."
And then there's another one going the same way and I
carry her, too.
Each time we walk another round in the neighborhood,
another squiggly amphibian wiggles her
tender body on rain drop feet making her way
one way or another
In the end, nine salamanders
airlifted to the
other side.
We go home to our houses.
Waving good-bye, she smiles and calls,
"See you tomorrow!"

Vivian Shipley Contest, 2021
Judge: Robert Cording

1st Prize
John Sibley Williams
"At This Table We Sing with Joy, with Sorrow"

2nd Prize
Matt Hohner
"This Poem Has Been Sanitized for Your Protection"

3rd Prize
Karen Holmberg
"As It Should Be"

About the Judge: Robert Cording has published nine collections of poems, the most recent of which are *Only So Far* and *Without My Asking* (CavanKerry Press). A book on poetry, the Bible and metaphor, *Finding the World's Fullness*, is out from Slant. He has received two National Endowment for the Arts Fellowships in poetry and has won a Pushcart Prize in poetry.

John Sibley Williams

First Prize, Vivian Shipley Award, 2021

At This Table We Sing with Joy, with Sorrow

for Sean Sherman, Oglala Lakota Sioux chef and cookbook author

If not for the body, let's rafter this old table up
like once-believed-in hymns simply for the sake of it.

Let's brush the dust of dead stars from the lacy cloth.
Scrape our plates free of what our grandparents failed

to finish & our children, hopefully, will never learn
to swallow. Every night it seems the worst of us

takes over & again the table sinks out of reach.
The glass always half-empty, and we empty it.

All this amaranth scattered across the floor so we can hear
our ghosts when they enter, & when they leave us. So much

unwilded rice & unprepared longing. How we cannot stop
mending what is not yet broken & killing to prove the world

still needs us. There are still so many unlit fires in our ovens,
sometimes I forget there's meant to be a difference between us

& them, between an unpainted & a burning cross. My daughters
carry my name like a cross over their tender little shoulders.

I no longer know what to say when asked for the truth.
Whose truth will keep the sorrow from their song?

Someone handcrafted this unvarnished oak so we might
one day take stock of one another. Let's prop our history up

on piles of unread books, so nothing wobbles, so the legs
grow equally tall, so even that uncle they say struggled

to hurt others the way he would never be hurt can join us,
all the ugliness intact, & his wife who conformed to her container

like goat milk. Let's sit, please, at this table between my own mixed-
race daughters & the hate you'd have had for them. Here's some crushed

berries for your toast. A dull knife to spread it. Outside nothing has changed
of the American sycamore apart from what we've chosen to hang from it.

Matt Hohner

Second Prize, Vivian Shipley Award, 2021

This Poem Has Been Sanitized for Your Protection

This poem is organic, macrobiotic, made with 100% recycled,
post-consumer language, and trigger-free. Surface meanings
have been scrubbed clean with disinfected phrasing. References
to sadness, massacres, mistreatment of people and Mother Nature
have been replaced with images of gentle, fluffy animals doing
cute things with babies. Theme and tone have been thoroughly
vetted by a panel of experts, clergy, and business leaders so as
not to threaten the status quo. Diction and syntax were generated
using renewable energy. All negative thoughts have been converted
to the American Dream. No one will die in this poem. Everyone will
go to heaven. Every word in this poem is a military or professional
sports hero. This poem can be played on any format radio station.
Reading this poem out loud replenishes rainforests and coral reefs.
Its carbon footprint is negative. Whales sing this poem to their young.
Whispering this poem resurrects forgotten tongues and extinct spe-
cies.
This poem is child-safe; none of its easily recognizable allusions
to western culture contain nuts, wheat, eggs, meat, gluten, sugar,
salt, pesticides, herbicides, or lactose. Your aunt from Des Moines
will ask you for a copy of this poem. Every metaphor is food-safe,
hypoallergenic, anti-microbial, and certified fair-trade. This poem
will never be censored on Facebook. These lines will be used in
speeches by kind and benevolent world leaders because no one can
argue with clean poems. This poem extols beautiful things without
being specific, because safe poems use words like *beautiful*
and everyone loves them. This poem will look good in a gold
frame on your living room wall. Read this poem at weddings
and funerals. You wish you wrote this poem, and you could have,
because it's safe, and good, and beautiful, and everyone loves it.

Karen Holmberg

Third Prize, *Vivian Shipley Award, 2021*

As It Should Be

Bleached reeds, shattered by the waves' delicate
insistence, tallied in lots of two or three,
are as they should be.

The light glazing the low knuckles on a cast
crab shell, turned ruddy as a nipple,
is as it should be.

The scrawl of leaf litter, mahogany brown,
a fine tobacco marking the tide's
highest grasp, is as it should be.

The brittle monarch tilting this way and that,
scudding an inch or two in puffs
of wind, is as it should be.

The salt tolerant plant, stem torqued and cracked
by footfalls, one leaf still reaching its torn palm
for the sun, is as it should be.

Whether it lives or dies
is as it should be.

They have taken up your minerals,
your elemental particles.
Because you are not

as you should be, your mind
riven by cancer's gall,
not as it should be.

Not as the whitened leaf
held afloat by the oak gall, sentenced
to an early fall in barely August.

Unless we can say, as the leaf would say,
so be it. Unless we can let you be
like the dying leaf,

replete: another cell
in the world's endless
unbuilding and rebuilding body.

Christine Beck

Three Recent Books by Connecticut Poets

Hindsight: 2020
author: Vivian Shipley
publisher: Louisiana Literature Press

God said it to Lot's Wife. Hades said it to Orpheus: "Don't Look Back." Really bad things, like being turned into a pillar of salt or losing your beloved to the underworld will happen if you look back. So, one might be tempted to view Vivian Shipley's latest book of poetry, *Hindsight: 2020*, as a dangerous endeavor, particularly as what's looming in the rearview mirror is the Covid pandemic that hit the world in 2020.

To begin with, most of us are thoroughly sick of talking about Covid. There is nothing remotely uplifting about looking back at where we've been since the pandemic began, particularly as we aren't sure where we are going next.

But those familiar with Shipley's work will find her signature style: a wry and engaging deep dive into the confluence of family and the natural world, coupled with an innate curiosity that results in inspiring poetry, even about death. Shipley wrestles with deaths both far back in hindsight and more current. From poems about witches hanged in the 1600s to her sister's recent death from brain cancer, Shipley unflinchingly examines what we love and those we lose. To be sure, Covid and its effects permeate many of her fine poems. In "No Rehearsal," she approaches Covid with a metaphor about writing poetry:

> What I fear is breath, living in a ventilator, will go on
> and on unlike a poem whose lines I can choose to end.

In her poem "Adrift," she uses the metaphor of rowing a dinghy to illustrate the conundrum of moving forward while looking back:

> I gave myself up to the illogical: to row the dinghy
> forward I had to face the stern. Backwards, I

could not see where I was headed…

Her poems about the death of her sister, to whom the book is dedicated, are poignant. Her sister died, not of Covid, but of a fourteen-year struggle with brain cancer. Yet, at the end, she was isolated due to Covid rules in her care facility so that Shipley could see her only through plexiglass. In "My Sister Isolated by Covid," Shipley writes:

> I'm unable to quarantine my heart as her lips sag
> when I tell her who I am.

These poems, clear-eyed about life and death, still brim with hope and humor. As with all of Shipley's work, her spirit shines through. In poems about teaching her granddaughter Isabella to swim, ice skate, and build a fort, Shipley contemplates the survival of the next generation.

In a delightful poem about punctuation called "Finals," Shipley bookmarks her retirement with a semicolon. The semicolon, it turns out, is an apt metaphor for the present—a time when the worst of Covid may be behind us, but we pause, not knowing what lies ahead. The poem ends:

> Not quite a stop but a strong pause,
> it's a link to a future offering me the rare
> opportunity to have life both ways.

Fortunately for us, Shipley has not been turned into a pillar of salt or suffered her beloved being banished to the underworld. The poems in *Hindsight: 2020* are a welcome addition to her body of distinguished work.

. . . .

The Rounding
author: Rennie McQuilkin
publisher: Antrim House

Rennie McQuilkin has done it again, which after nineteen books of poetry, a bout with severe illness, selling his country farmhouse, and relocating to a retirement facility, is an extraordinary achievement. The Poet Laureate of Connecticut from 2015 to 2017, McQuilkin continues his book of days, reflecting on the natural world and his sheer delight in the creatures he observes. His sense of humor abounds and we delight with him.

The Rounding is a series of short poems that picks up from July 2020, where his previous book left off. Written during the pandemic, there is no hint of being locked down, locked in or unable to bask in the delight of the natural world. When McQuilkin invokes "bestial attention," we recognize for him, it is an invocation to the holy.

Linking the natural world to childhood brings special pleasure. In "Murder in the Glen," the residents of his retirement home discover a dead rabbit, which prompts a debate as to the murderer—rat, weasel or mink. Remembering his grandmother's mink stole, baleful gaze of its glass eye peering at him in church, he hopes the murderer was a mink, an animal of fearful beauty:

> Maybe we elders remember the mink
> stoles our grandmothers wore to church, their velvety
> softness we touched when our grannies returned
> from drinking the blood and eating the flesh.
>
> That was called communion, and the mink a lovely
> part of it. We know better than to wear animal pelts
> around our necks now, but the memory lingers.
> Let it be a mink that did it, fed its young.
>
> May we too go in no less style.
> May it not be the plague that takes us by the throat
> when our time is up, but something whose bestiality
> allows us to find a kind of fearful beauty in it.

In "Suspension," McQuilkin links birds to the souls of the departed, in a particularly poignant poem:

> Strange how it always seems to happen.
> A heron stands in for my departed father,
> looking my way insistently, not minding

its own business that first day without him

McQuilkin is at heart an educator, a student of the habits of creatures, an apologist for what might seem bestial behavior. In "For the Giant Pacific Octopus," he draws us to its playful nature:

> Like all wild things, it kills only to survive.
> In its off-hours the octopus loves
> to play and will dance with the same fish
> it ate that morning.

We sense McQuillen playing and dancing throughout this collection. Like the image of the orangutan, circling its kin to keep them warm, we long to hold McQuilkin with his insouciant charm a little longer, as he embraces his family:

> The orangutan and I might as well be brothers,
> so humped and crippled am I, and always cold,
> my toes curled, discolored and numb.
> But I too am blessed.
> Like his, my children have rushed in
> and secured a safe perch for this old simian.
> I feel their arms around me.

Anyone who has heard McQuilkin read aloud recalls his gravelly voice, the laughter that bubbles in his readings. Have a listen on YouTube. And enjoy this latest offering from one of our poetry elders.

. . . .

The Glass Globe
author: Margaret Gibson
LSU Press

Margaret Gibson, whose term as Poet Laureate of the state of Connecticut ended in June 2022, has released the third book in a trilogy about her husband's diagnosis, illness, and death from Alzheimer's. Yet *The Glass Globe* paints on a large canvas that encompasses may facets of loss and grief, including grief for the future of the world.

Gibson took as her special mission as Poet Laureate issues of climate change and the destruction facing the earth, reading at "green cafes" around the state. Gibson has recently remarked that for years, she felt diminished when referred to as a "nature poet." Today, she says she wears the title with pride if it means being a poet concerned with the future of the natural world.

The image of a glass globe presents a metaphor for the broken earth. The actual glass globe is a glass globe that sits in her bay window as a prism to the outdoors. Gibson braids into her poem words she wrote in an essay about the globe years ago with a current meditation on the fact that it has cracked:

> Except for me, everyone who came to my wedding is
> dead. I'm in another house now. The glass globe rests in
>   another
> morning's light.
> . . .
> Live with it
> that way,
>   love it, love it crazed
>
> and cracked, love it broken. Because everything, everything
> already is. Broken.

One of her most beautifully braided poems, "Wing," begins with an image of an owl's wing given by a neighbor. Somewhat appalled, she meditates on words that lie within other words, such as *flow* that lies inside *flower* or the word *art* that lies inside *heart*. The poem moves to a meditation on a friend who killed himself by drowning and then returns to words:

> And yes…I will seize on words, I will fall
> silently on them
>
> and hold them down in a steady grasp
> and open them
>
> I will feed this hunger to know that inside

know
        is now.

The beauty of Gibson's work is that every poem, whether about the natural world or the death of a loved one, circles back to an expansive embodiment of grief, grief in an owl's wing, a friend's suicide, or her husband's death.

In her poem "Asides and Notations," Gibson speaks eloquently to her grief for the world in a section called "Climate":

> Surely someone will devise
> an isotherm
>
> for grief, once the shearing-off
> from ice sheets
>
> In Antarctica and Greenland
> erases coastal
>
> wetlands cities rivers fields
> and reservoirs—that is
>
> when elsewhere is tangibly here
> and we can taste it
>
> flavoring the water for coffee once
> served streaming
>
> in outdoor cafes in what we remember
> as Amsterdam
>
> Cape Town, San Francisco, Rio.

In lesser hands, a book on grief might be depressing or fit fare only for those experiencing loss, but Gibson is not a lesser poet. Her work sparkles with intelligence and wit, inviting us to see the world through the lens of a cracked glass globe, damaged yet still beautiful.

Connecticut Poetry Society Contests

The Connecticut Poetry Society offers five annual poetry contests, two of which are open only to Connecticut residents.

CPS board members are not eligible to enter contests.

Contest Winners must wait a year before entering again.

MARGARET GIBSON POET LAUREATE POETRY AWARD

for a poem on nature in a time of global climate crisis

Open to all poets
Opens: March 1
Deadline: April 15

Submit up to 3 pages of previously unpublished poems, any form
Prizes: 1st – $300; 2nd – $200; 3rd – $100
No submission fee is required.

Winning poems will be published in *Connecticut River Review* and posted on the Connecticut Poetry Society website. Winners receive a free, two-year membership in the Connecticut Poetry Society.

Simultaneous submissions are acceptable; however, please notify us immediately upon acceptance elsewhere.

This contest is for poems that focus mindfully on the living world during this time of global climate crisis. Such poems are called by various names: climate crisipoetry, eco-poetry, nature poetry, "green" poetry. We are looking for poems that explore experiences of the natural world—remembering that the natural and human are connected by patterns of reciprocity as well as impacted by human choices and actions that may be social, economic, political, or spiritual.

We welcome poems from poets of every racial and cultural background and experience: we all live on this earth together.
Final Judge: Margaret Gibson, Connecticut Poet Laureate Emerita

Electronic Submissions Only
Submit at: www.connecticutriverreview.submittable.com.

Submit up to three previously unpublished poems in one document, no more than one poem per page. No contact info on poems (contact information will be requested separately via Submittable).

Guidelines are available on the CPS website: www.ctpoetry.net

CONNECTICUT POETRY AWARD

In honor of Connecticut Poetry Society founders,
Wallace Winchell, Ben Brodine, and Joseph Brodinsky

Open to all poets
Opens: April 1
Deadline: May 31

Fee $15 for up to 3 unpublished poems, any form, 80-line limit
Prizes: 1st – $400; 2nd – $100; 3rd – $50

Winning poems will be published in *Connecticut River Review* and posted on the Connecticut Poetry Society website.

Winners receive a free, two-year membership in the Connecticut Poetry Society.

Simultaneous submissions are acceptable; however,
please notify us immediately upon acceptance elsewhere.

Electronic Submissions Only
Submit at: www.connecticutriverreview.submittable.com.

Submit up to three previously unpublished poems in one document, no more than one poem per page; 80-line limit. No contact info on poems (contact information will be requested separately via Submittable).

Guidelines are available on the CPS website: www.ctpoetry.net

EXPERIMENTAL POETRY CONTEST

Open to all poets
Opens: June 15
Deadline: July 31

Fee $15 for up to 3 unpublished poems
First Prize is $1,000
Up to four finalists will also be identified.

Winning poem will be published in *Connecticut River Review* and posted on the Connecticut Poetry Society website.

Winners receive a free, two-year membership in the Connecticut Poetry Society.

Submit up to three poems; text, audio and video files are acceptable. Submissions may include poems composed using 1) an entirely new form; 2) an existing form that is considered experimental; or 3) a radical subversion of a traditional form.

No identifying information should go on the file (contact information will be requested separately via Submittable).

Simultaneous submissions are acceptable; however, please notify us immediately upon acceptance elsewhere.

Electronic Submissions Only
Submit at: www.connecticutriverreview.submittable.com.

Guidelines are available on the CPS website: www.ctpoetry.net

THE VIVIAN SHIPLEY POETRY AWARD

Open to all poets
Opens: August 1
Deadline: September 30

Fee $15 for up to 3 unpublished poems, any form, 80-line limit
Prizes: 1st – $1,000; 2nd – $100; 3rd – $50

Winning poems will be published in *Connecticut River Review* and posted on the Connecticut Poetry Society website.

Winners receive a free, two-year membership in the Connecticut Poetry Society.

Simultaneous submissions are acceptable; however,
please notify us immediately upon acceptance elsewhere.

Electronic Submissions Only
Submit at: www.connecticutriverreview.submittable.com.

Submit up to three previously unpublished poems in one document, no more than one poem per page; 80-line limit. No contact info on poems (contact information will be requested separately via Submittable).

Guidelines are available on the CPS website: www.ctpoetry.net

NUTMEG POETRY AWARD

Open to Connecticut poets only
Opens: December 1
Deadline: January 31

Fee: Members of CPS may enter this contest without paying a fee; for non-members the fee is $10.

Prizes: 1st – $200; 2nd – $100; 3rd – $50

Winning poems will be posted on the Connecticut Poetry Society website.

Winners receive a free, two-year membership in the Connecticut Poetry Society.

Simultaneous submissions are acceptable; however, please notify us immediately upon acceptance elsewhere.

Electronic Submissions Only
Submit at: www.connecticutriverreview.submittable.com.

Submit up to three previously unpublished poems, in one document, no more than one poem per page; 80-line limit. No contact info on poems (contact information will be requested separately via Submittable).

Guidelines are available on the CPS website: www.ctpoetry.net

LYNN DECARO POETRY COMPETITION

In memory of Lynn DeCaro, a promising young Connecticut Poetry Society member who died of leukemia in 1986

made possible through the generous support of
the Betty and Allen DeCaro Family

Open to Connecticut student poets in grades 9-12
Opens: January 1
Deadline: March 15

Prizes: 1st – $100; 2nd – $50; 3rd – $25

No fee for up to 3 unpublished poems, 40-line limit

Winning poems will be posted on the Connecticut Poetry Society website. Winners receive a free, two-year membership in the Connecticut Poetry Society.

Simultaneous submissions are acceptable; however, please notify us immediately upon acceptance elsewhere.

Electronic Submissions Only
Submit at: www.connecticutriverreview.submittable.com.

Submit up to three previously unpublished poems, in one document, no more than one poem per page. No contact info on poems (contact information will be requested separately via Submittable).

Guidelines are available on the CPS website: www.ctpoetry.net

CONTRIBUTOR NOTES

Connecticut River Review
extends its sincere appreciation
to all its contributors.

Liz Abrams-Morley's collections include *Beholder*, 2018, Inventory, 2014, and *Necessary Turns* (published by Word Poetry in 2010, winner of the 2010 Eric Hoffer Award for Excellence in Small Press Publishing). In 2020, she was named the *Passager* Poet in *Passager Journal*'s annual contest. Abrams-Morley is co-founder of Around the Block Writers' Collaborative (www.aroundtheblockwriters.org).

Brian Wallace Baker holds an MFA from Western Kentucky University and lives in Tooele, Utah, with his wife and daughter. His writing has appeared in *Little Patuxent Review, River Teeth's Beautiful Things* column, *Split Lip Magazine, Whale Road Review*, and elsewhere. You can find him on Twitter @bbrianwallace.

makalani bandele is an Affrilachian Poets and Cave Canem fellow. He has also received fellowships from the Kentucky Arts Council, Millay Colony, and Vermont Studio Center. He holds an MFA from the University of Kentucky. His work has been published in several anthologies and widely in literary journals. The author of *hellfightin'* and *under the aegis of a winged mind*, his poems have been most recently published in *Poetry Northwest, Ovenbird*, and *The Common*.

Christine Beck holds an MFA from Southern Connecticut State University and is the author of *Blinding Light* (Grayson Books, 2013), *I'm Dating Myself* (Dancing Girl Press, 2015), *Stirred, Not Shaken* (Five Oaks Press, 2016), and the book of poetry and prompts *Beneath the Steps: A Writing Guide for 12-Step Recovery*. She is a former president of Connecticut Poetry Society and was Poet Laureate of the town of West Hartford, Connecticut from 2015-17. Find more information at www.ChristineBeck.net.

Erica Bernheim currently teaches literature and writing at Florida Southern College, where she also directs the creative writing program and curates a Visiting Writers Series. Her full-length collection, *The Mimic Sea*, was published by 42 Miles Press (Indiana University South Bend). Her creative and critical work has recently appeared or is forthcoming in *Kestrel, Bennington Review, DIAGRAM*, and *The Kenyon Review*.

Sherri Bedingfield is the author of two poetry collections: *Transitions and Transformations* (Antrim House, 2010) and *The Clattering: Voices from Old Forfarshire Scotland* (Grayson Books, 2016). Her work appears in many journals and anthologies, including *Connecticut River Review, Our Changing Environment,* and *Civilization in Crisis.* Bedingfield is on the Board of Riverwood Poetry Series at Real Art Ways in Hartford, Connecticut and has served as co-host for the Wintonbury Library Poetry Series in Bloomfield, Connecticut. Bedingfield is a licensed family therapist.

Nick Bertelson is a farmer from Southwestern Iowa. His work has appeared in multiple journals. He is a James Hearst Poetry Prize finalist and author of *Harvest Widows* (North Dakota State University Press, 2019).

Laura Bonazzoli's poetry has appeared in dozens of literary magazines, including *Naugatuck River Review, Northern New England Review,* and *SLANT,* as well as in four anthologies and on "Poems from Here" on Maine Public Radio. She has also published personal essays and fiction. Her collection of linked short stories, *Consecration Pond,* is forthcoming from Toad Hall Editions in September of 2022. She is online at laurabonazzoli.com.

Michael McKeown Bondhus (formerly Charlie) is a bigender (male/neutrois) Irish American writer. He's the author of *Divining Bones* (Sundress, 2018) and *All the Heat We Could Carry* (Main Street Rag, 2013), winner of the Thom Gunn Award. His work has appeared in *Poetry, Poetry Ireland Review, Missouri Review, Columbia Journal, Hayden's Ferry Review,* and others. Formerly of Connecticut, he now lives in Jersey City, New Jersey (Lenape land) and teaches at Raritan Valley Community College. More at: http://michaelbondhus.com

Roxanne Cardona was born in New York City of Puerto Rican heritage. She has poems published or forthcoming in *One Art: A Journal of Poetry, Mason Street, Constellations, Red Eft Review, Writing in a Woman's Voice, Poetic Medicine-New Voices,* and elsewhere. She has a BA/MS from Hunter College, and an MS from College of New Rochelle. She was an elementary school teacher and principal in the South Bronx.

Susana H. Case has authored eight books of poetry, most recently *The Damage Done*, (Broadstone Books, 2022). Her book *Dead Shark on the N Train* (Broadstone Books, 2020) won a Pinnacle Book Award for Best Poetry Book, a New York City Big Book Award Distinguished Favorite, and was a finalist for the Eric Hoffer Book Award. She co-edited, with Margo Taft Stever, *I Wanna Be Loved by You: Poems on Marilyn Monroe* (Milk and Cake Press, 2022). http://www.susanahcase.com/

Lucia Cherciu writes both in English and in Romanian and is the author of five books of poetry, including *Train Ride to Bucharest* (Sheep Meadow Press, 2017), a winner of the Eugene Paul Nassar Poetry Prize. She is the 2021 Dutchess County Poet Laureate, and her work was nominated three times for a Pushcart Prize and twice for Best of the Net. She teaches English at SUNY/Dutchess Community College. Her web page is http://luciacherciu.webs.com. @CherciuLucia

Paula Colangelo's poems are published in *SWWIM Every Day*, *Lily Poetry Review*, *Connotation Press: An Online Artifact* and forthcoming in *Sugar House Review*, *Amethyst Review* and *Canary Literary Magazine*. Her book reviews appear in *Pleiades* and *Rain Taxi*. She received an MFA in Poetry from Drew University and has taught poetry in healing focused rehabilitation programs.

Taylor Lynn Copeland is an emerging poet from Northeastern Connecticut who, after many years of writing in various genres, is now seeking to publish her poetry. She is a member of the Connecticut Poetry Society and a winner of the Julius Sokenu Poetry Awards. Copeland participates in a workshop group, and recently had a piece published in the *Woodstock Villager*.

Robert Cording's ninth book of poetry, *Without My Asking*, was a runner up for the Connecticut Book Award. His tenth book of poems, *In the Unwalled City*, is due in 2022 from Slant Books. He has work forthcoming in *The Common*, *Poetry Northwest*, *Hudson Review*, *Southern Review*, *32 Poems*, *Image*, and *The Sun*.

Jennifer Cox is a poet, lawyer, and mother. Her poetry primarily revolves around motherhood, birth, and the impending climate crisis. She enjoys reading, spending time outdoors, and playing with her children. Her work has previously appeared in the League of Canadian Poets' *Poetry Pause* and *Bywords*. She resides in Ottawa with her children and husband.

Oluwasegun Isaac Daramola is a Nigerian poet. He has been published in literary magazines such as *LitQuarterly, Lumin Journal, Pithead Chapel Magazine,* among others. He was a recipient of the 2020 *SprinNG* poetry fellowship.

Annie Diamond is a poet, Joycean, and breakfast enthusiast living and working on the traditional unceded homelands of the Council of the Three Fires. She has been awarded fellowships by MacDowell, Luminarts Cultural Foundation, The Lighthouse Works, and Boston University, where she earned her MFA and taught creative writing in 2017. Her poems have appeared or are forthcoming in *No Tokens, Yemassee, Rabbit Catastrophe Review, Western Humanities Review,* and elsewhere.

Marc Alan Di Martino is a Pushcart-nominated poet, translator, and author of the collections *Unburial* (Kelsay, 2019) and *Still Life with City* (Pski's Porch, 2022). His work appears in *Palette Poetry, Rattle, Rust + Moth, Tinderbox, Valparaiso Poetry Review* and many other journals and anthologies. Currently a poetry reader for the *Baltimore Review,* he lives in Italy.

Thomas Festa is a Professor of English at the State University of New York, New Paltz, and the author of a forthcoming chapbook of poems, *Earthen* (Finishing Line Press). Other recent and forthcoming work includes an ecopoetic reading of W.S. Merwin's late poetry (in *ISLE: Interdisciplinary Studies in Literature and Environment* 21.1) and poems in *Bennington Review, Contemporary Haibun Online, Drifting Sands Haibun, Poetry Quarterly,* and *Stone Poetry Journal.*

James Finnegan has published poems in *Ploughshares, Poetry Northwest, The Southern Review, The Virginia Quarterly Review,* as well as in the anthologies: *Good Poems: American Places* edited by Garrison Keillor; *Laureates of Connecticut; Shadows of Unfinished Things;*

Imagining Vesalius; Waking Up to the Earth: Connecticut Poets in a time of Global Climate Crisis; and recently *Walkers in the City.* For over a decade he served as president of the Friends & Enemies of Wallace Stevens (stevenspoetry.org). He posts aphoristic ars poetica on the blog *ursprache*: https://ursprache.blogspot.com/

Marsha Foss, a retired educator, divides her time between her two favorite states, Minnesota and Maryland. When in St. Paul, she enjoys being connected to the area's vibrant writing community. Her work has been published in numerous online and print journals, and she has been nominated for a Pushcart Prize. An added joy is living near young grandsons.

Jennifer L. Freed lives in Massachusetts. Her poems have appeared in *Atlanta Review, Atticus Review, The Worcester Review, Zone 3,* and others, and have received Pushcart and *Orison Anthology* nominations. Awards include the 2020 Samuel Washington Allen Prize. Her full-length collection, *When Light Shifts* (Kelsay, 2022), explores the aftermath of her mother surviving a cerebral hemorrhage. More at jfreed.weebly.com

Louis Gabordi is a retired educator and mentor to young poets. His work has been recognized by the New Millenium Writing Awards and published in the anthology *Waking Up to the Earth: Connecticut Poets in a time of Global Climate Crisis.* Nothing so informs his work as his love, concern, and respect for the natural world. He lives in Ledyard, Connecticut, with his spouse and writing partner Catherine DeNunzio.

Margaret Gibson, Poet Laureate of Connecticut, has published thirteen books of poems, most recently *The Glass Globe.* She is the recipient of The Lamont Selection, Melville Kane Award, and Connecticut Book Award, a Finalist for the National Book Award, and for the Poets' Prize. With a grant from the Academy of American Poets, she edited an anthology, *Waking Up to the Earth: Connecticut Poets in a Time of Global Climate Crisis.* Visit her website at www.MargaretGibsonPoetry.com.

Cindy Glovinsky grew up in Des Moines, Iowa, and now lives in Ann Arbor, Michigan. She has published poems and stories in *Ploughshares* (as Cynthia Housh), *Aries, Barbaric Yawp, Bear River Review, The Chaffin Journal, Plainsong,* and *Pacific Coast Journal.* She also published three non-fiction books with St. Martin's Press, and a memoir, *Music, Lakes & Blue Corduroy,* with Thunder Bay Press in Michigan.

Kristina Hakanson is a graduate of Pacific University's MFA in Writing program. Recent poems of hers have appeared in *Basin Bards 44 Poets: A Klamath Anthology, Reunion: The Dallas Review, ellipsis...,* and *NonBinary Review.* Her chapbook, *The Holy or the Broken Hallelujah,* was published in 2022 by Finishing Line Press. She lives in Arizona. logic0fwings.wordpress.com

Paul Hamill, a former college professor and administrator, lived on a farm in upstate New York and recently moved to Hartford, Connecticut. He is the author of four collections of poetry and the prose book *And Crown thy Good with Brotherhood: On the Imagination of Fraternity* (Amazon, 2019). He has poems published in journals, most recently *Georgia Review* and *Cumberland River Review.*

Shellie Harwood is a Connecticut poet, actress, and playwright. Her poetry has appeared in *TulipTree Review, Oberon, Mudfish22,* and *Sixfold Poetry.* She won the 2022 Nutmeg Poetry Award for her poem "Afterswarm" and received Honorable Mention in the Vivian Shipley Poetry Award. The title poem of Shellie's chapbook, *With My Sister, in a Tornado Warning* (Finishing Line Press, 2021), received the 2021 Oberon Herbert Poetry Prize. Her chapbook, *Sleepwalker's Guide to Grieving,* is forthcoming in 2023.

Judd Hess holds an MFA and an MA from Chapman University. He has won the Fugue Poetry Prize, the John Fowles Creative Writing Prize for Poetry, the Ellipsis Prize; and has been nominated for the Pushcart Prize. His work most recently has appeared in *Cathexis Northwest Press, Philadelphia Stories,* and *Temenos,* and won Honorable Mention in the 2021 Ellen Conroy Kennedy Poetry Contest.

Maggie Rue Hess is an educator currently living with her husband and two dogs in Knoxville, Tennessee. Her poetry has previously appeared in *Rattle*, the *Minnesota Review*, and several other publications. When she isn't speed reading, she might be found baking or going to trivia nights with friends.

Laura Reece Hogan is the author of *Litany of Flights* (Paraclete Press, 2020), winner of the Paraclete Poetry Prize, the chapbook *O Garden-Dweller* (Finishing Line Press), and the nonfiction book *I Live, No Longer I* (Wipf & Stock). She is one of ten poets featured in the anthology *In a Strange Land* (Cascade Books). Her poems have appeared or are forthcoming in *RHINO*, *Scientific American*, *Rust + Moth*, *Cloudbank*, and other publications. www.laurareecehogan.com

Matt Hohner is an editor for *Loch Raven Review*. His work has appeared in *The Moth*, *takahē*, *Prairie Schooner*, *New Contrast*, *Narrative Magazine*, and many other publications. Hohner's first collection of poetry, *Thresholds and Other Poems*, was published by Apprentice House in 2018. His second poetry collection is forthcoming from Salmon Poetry in 2023. He lives in Baltimore, Maryland.

Karen Holmberg is the author of two full length collections of poems; the second, *Axis Mundi*, was named one of the top poetry titles of 2013 by *Slate*. Holmberg also publishes lyric essays, with recent ones appearing in *Tupelo Quarterly* and *Briar Cliff Review*. She teaches in the MFA program at Oregon State.

Tony Howarth, editor for dramatic writing with *The Westchester Review*, is a playwright, director, and former journalist. He retired in 1991 after 28 years as a high school and college teacher of English and theatre. Howarth began writing poetry in 2009 after a visit to William Wordsworth's Dove Cottage (and his daffodils) in England's Lake District.

Heather Jessen is a 2021 finalist for the Ruminate broadside prize and the *Atlanta Review* poetry contest. She has an MFA in writing for children from Simmons University and an MA in social work from the University of Chicago. A former resident of Australia, she currently lives in Connecticut.

Frederick-Douglass Knowles II is a Professor of English at Three Rivers Community College in his native city of Norwich, Connecticut, and is the inaugural Poet Laureate of Hartford. He is the recipient of the Nutmeg Poetry Award and the Connecticut of The Arts Fellow in Artist Excellence for Poetry/Creative Non-Fiction. Knowles is a two-time Pushcart Prize nominee and the author of *BlackRoseCity*.

Susannah Lawrence lives in northwest Connecticut, the rocky part. Her collection, *Just Above the Bone*, appeared in 2016. She holds an MFA in Writing from Vermont College of Fine Arts. Her work has appeared in *Nimrod*, *The Cortland Review*, *The MacGuffin*, *Poet Lore*, *The Comstock Review*, *Green Hills Literary Lantern*, and, most recently, the anthology *Waking Up to the Earth: Connecticut Poets in a Time of Global Climate Crisis*.

Jeffrey Letterly is a composer and multi-disciplined performer. He was born and raised in the heartland of the Midwest and now resides in Syracuse, New York. His poetry appears in *Atticus Review*, *Bird Brained Zine Anthology*, *BOMBFIRE*, *The Comstock Review*, *Pif Magazine*, *Sip Cup*, *Stone Canoe*, and other places.

Richard Levine is a retired New York City teacher and the author of *Richard Levine: Selected Poems*, *Contiguous States*, and five chapbooks. *Now in Contest* is forthcoming from Fernwood Press. He was co-editor of *Invasion of Ukraine 2022: Poems*. He is also an Advisory Editor to *BigCityLit.com*. Website: richardlevine107.com

David Lloyd is the author of ten books, including three poetry collections: *Warriors* (2012), *The Gospel According to Frank* (2009), and *The Everyday Apocalypse* (2002). In 2000, he received the Poetry Society of America's Robert H. Winner Award, judged by W. D. Snodgrass. His articles, interviews, poems, and stories have appeared in numerous journals including *Crab Orchard Review*, *Denver Quarterly*, *TriQuarterly*, and *Virginia Quarterly Review*. He directs the Creative Writing Program at Le Moyne College.

Melissa McKinstry earned her MFA in poetry at Pacific University. Her work has appeared in *Rattle* and *Alaska Quarterly Review*, earned honorable mention for the Steve Kowit Poetry Prize as well as contests at *Crab Creek Review* and *The Comstock Review*, and is forthcoming in *december*.

Rennie McQuilkin has served as Connecticut Poet Laureate (2015-2018). He co-founded the Sunken Garden Poetry Festival, which he directed for nine years. His poetry has appeared in *The Atlantic, Poetry, The American Scholar, The Southern Review*, and elsewhere. The author of several poetry collections, his awards include fellowships from the National Endowment for the Arts and the Connecticut Commission on the Arts, the Connecticut Center for the Book's Lifetime Achievement Award, and its 2010 poetry award.

Dan Murphy teaches at Boston University. He previously served as Writer-in-Residence at Phillips Academy. His poems have appeared, or will appear, in *Sugar House Review, The Adirondack Review, The Summerset Review, Terrain, Slipstream* and elsewhere.

Meryl Natchez's fourth book, *Catwalk,* received an Indie Best Book 2020 Award from *Kirkus Reviews.* Natchez' work has appeared or is forthcoming in *Alaska Quarterly Review, LA Review of Books, Hudson Review, Poetry Northwest, Literary Matters, The American Journal of Poetry, Tupelo Quarterly, ZYZZYVA,* and others. She is Chair of Marin Poetry Center and blogs at www.merylnatchez.com.

Peter O'Donovan is a scientist and writer living in Seattle, Washington. Originally from the Canadian prairies, he received his doctorate from the University of Toronto, studying design aesthetics. His poetry has appeared or is forthcoming in *New Ohio Review, Atlanta Review, Qwerty, River Heron Review, Typehouse Literary Magazine*, and elsewhere.

Kurt Olsson's work has appeared in a wide variety of publications, including *Poetry, The Threepenny Review, The New Republic,* and *Southern Review.* He has published two collections of poetry, *Burning Down Disneyland* (Gunpowder Press) and *What Kills What Kills Us* (Silverfish Review Press).

S.E. Page has an M.S. and certification in Secondary English and is the co-editor of *Young Ravens Literary Review*. A Pushcart Prize nominee, her poems have been published in journals including *Connecticut River Review, Fresh Ink, Star*Line, Noctua Review,* and *Oakwood*. As a child she dearly wished her first initial stood for something adventurous and dashing like Seraphina or Sapphira, but she has grown comfortable with being a Sarah. Discover more about her ink at iffymagic.com.

Ryan Parker's mission, as an educator in Manchester, Connecticut, for over 20 years, is to disrupt the oppressive legacy embedded in educational spaces and to influence and empower educators and youth to also engage in the disruption. In addition to his work as an educator, Parker is a mama's boy, husband, father, brother, hip hop head and verbal artist who invests necessary time in tangling himself and others in poetry.

Marge Piercy has written twenty volumes of poetry, most recently *On the Way Out, Turn Off the Light* (Knopf, 2020) and *Made in Detroit* (Knopf, 2017). She is the author of seventeen novels, including *Sex War* (her most recent), *The New York Times* Bestseller *Gone To Soldiers,* the National Bestsellers *Braided Lives,* and *The Longings of Women;* her critically acclaimed memoir is *Sleeping with Cats*. She has given readings, workshops, and speeches at more than 570 venues.

Carol Potter is a Vermont resident brought up on a dairy farm in Northwestern Connecticut. She is the 2021 winner of the Pacific Coast Poetry series from *Beyond Baroque* for her sixth book of poems, *What Happens Next is Anyone's Guess*. She teaches for the Antioch University Low-Residency MFA program in Los Angeles and conducts private poetry workshops. For further information, please see her website, cwpotterverse.com.

Geri Radacsi is the author of five collections of poetry, including her prize-winning chapbook, *Ancient Music* (Pecan Grove Press, 2000) and her full-length poetry collection, *Trapped in Amber* (Connecticut River Press, 2005); Her latest collection, *My Oarsman* (Antrim House, 2021) is a tribute to the passing of her husband of 54 years. She is Associate Director of University Relations, Emerita, at Central Connecticut

State University. Her publishing credits include the *Atlanta Review*, *Comstock Review*, and *The MacGuffin*.

James Ragan has authored ten books (Grove/Atlantic, Henry Holt, U. of Oklahoma Press, Salmon Press), with work published in *Poetry*, *The Nation*, *L.A. Times*, *NAR*, *Epoch*, *World Lit. Today*, and *Poetry Ireland*, and appearing in fifteen languages and thirty-two anthologies. His plays *Commedia* and *Saints* have been staged in the United States, Moscow, Beijing, and Athens. He is the subject of the Arina Films documentary, *Flowers and Roots*, which was awarded seventeen Festival recognitions.

Lindsay Rockwell is currently the Poet-in-Residence for the Episcopal Church of Connecticut as well as host for their Poetry and Social Justice Dialogue series. She won first prize in the October Project Poetry Contest and the 81st Moon Prize from *Writing in a Woman's Voice*. She has been published in *Amethyst Review*, *Iron Horse Literary Review*, and *Birmingham Arts Journal*, among others. Rockwell also holds a Master of Dance and Choreography from NYU's Tisch School of the Arts.

Edwin Romond's most recent collection is *Home Team: Poems About Baseball* (Grayson Books). He has received a fellowship from the National Endowment for the Arts and won the 2013 New Jersey Poetry Prize for his poem, "Champion." His poems have twice been featured on NPR's *Writer's Almanac*. He lives in Wind Gap, Pennsylvania, with his wife and son.

Rikki Santer's poems have appeared in various publications including *Ms. Magazine*, *Poetry East*, *Heavy Feather Review*, *Slab*, *Slipstream*, *[PANK]*, *Crab Orchard Review*, *RHINO*, *Grimm*, *Hotel Amerika*, and *The Main Street Rag*. Her honors include six Pushcart and three Ohioana and Ohio Poet book award nominations, as well as a fellowship from the National Endowment for the Humanities. Her tenth collection, *How to Board a Moving Ship*, has just been released by Lily Poetry Review Books.

Maria Sassi, the inaugural Poet Laureate of West Hartford, Connecticut, is a prize-winning poet and playwright, and a long-time sponsor of a reading series at the Noah Webster House. Her books include *Rooted in Stars* and *Rare Grasses*. For years, Sassi taught creative writing at Hartford College for Women. Her video, *Five Ocean Poems*, was distributed to institutions throughout Connecticut. Her work has been much anthologized and published in literary journals, and she has read extensively throughout the Northeast.

Ellen Hirning Schmidt submitted her poems for the first time at age 70, less than four years ago. Since then, she has received the Helen Kay Chapbook Prize and a Pushcart nomination. Her work has also appeared in *Passager, The Avocet, Poetry Quarterly, Caesura, Blood & Thunder*, and elsewhere. She leads workshops in Ithaca, New York; Cornell University; and Star Island, New Hampshire. She is grateful for this award and to become a part of Connecticut Poetry Society. www.WritingRoomWorkshops.com

James Scruton is the author, most recently, of *The Rules* (Green Linden Press, 2019), and he has work in current or forthcoming issues of *Glimpse, Iconoclast, Kitchen Table Quarterly, Molecule*, and *Southern Poetry Review*. He is a Professor of English and Associate Academic Dean at Bethel University in McKenzie, Tennessee.

Vivian Shipley's thirteenth book is *Hindsight: 2020*, (Louisiana Literature, 2022). She won Naugatuck Valley Community College's 2022 Luke Newton Award, *The MacGuffin*'s 2020-21 Poet Hunt, and *Rattle*'s 10/2020 Ekphrastic Challenge. *An Archaeology of Days* (2019) was 2020-21 Paterson Poetry Prize Finalist and 2020 Housatonic Book Prize Finalist. *The Poet* and *Perennial* were published in 2015. *All of Your Messages Have Been Erased* won 2011's Paterson Literary Award, NEPC's Sheila Motton Book Award, and Connecticut Press Club's Prize.

Tara Skurtu is a two-time Fulbright grantee and recipient of a Robert Pinsky Global Fellowship and two Academy of American Poets prizes. She is the founder of International Poetry Circle, a steering committee member of Writers for Democratic Action, and works as a writing coach. Skurtu is the author of *The Amoeba Game* and the upcoming collection *Faith Farm*. Her poems have appeared in *Salmagundi*, *The Kenyon Review*, *Plume*, and *Poetry Wales*.

John L. Stanizzi is the author of ten books of poetry, including *Four Bits, Chants, Sundowning, POND*, and *The Tree That Lights the Way Home*. Besides *Connecticut River Review*, John's poems are published in *Prairie Schooner, Cortland Review, American Life in Poetry*, and elsewhere. John's nonfiction has appeared in *Literature and Belief, Stone Coast Review*, and elsewhere. He was awarded an Artist Fellowship in Creative Non-Fiction, 2021 from the Connecticut Office of the Arts. https://www.johnlstanizzi.com

Samn Stockwell has published in *Agni, Ploughshares*, and *The New Yorker*, among others. Her two books, *Theater of Animals* and *Recital*, won the National Poetry Series (USA) and the Editor's Prize at *Elixir*, respectively. Recent poems are published in *On the Seawall* and *Sugar House Review* and are forthcoming in Plume and elsewhere.

John Struloeff is the author of *The Man I Was Supposed to Be* (Loom Press) and *The Work of a Genius* (Finishing Line Press) and has published poems in *The Atlantic, The Sun, Verse Daily, The Southern Review, Prairie Schooner, ZYZZYVA, PN Review*, and elsewhere. He is a former Stegner and NEA Fellow and now directs the creative writing program at Pepperdine University.

John Surowiecki has written fourteen books of poetry; his most recent is *The Place of the Solitaires: Poems from Titles by Wallace Stevens* (Wolfson, 2022). His prizes include the Poetry Foundation's Pegasus Award for Verse Drama, the *Nimrod* Pablo Neruda Prize, the Washington Prize, a Connecticut Poetry Fellowship, and the Silver Medal in the Sunken Garden National Competition. His novel *Pie Man* won the 2017 Nilson Prize for a First Novel. His poems have been published widely.

Matthew Thorburn is the author of six books of poetry, including *The Grace of Distance*, a finalist for the Paterson Poetry Prize, and *Dear Almost*, which received the Lascaux Prize. His new book, *String*, is forthcoming from Louisiana State University Press in 2023. He lives in New Jersey.

Carol Was is the past Poetry Editor for *The MacGuffin*. She also worked in the fossil lab at Cranbrook Institute of Science. Fishing trips with her father, spending time on a family farm, and camp counseling special needs children helped shape her appreciation for the natural world. Her work has appeared in numerous journals including *The Gettysburg Review*, *The Southern Review*, and *The Connecticut Review*.

Pamela Wax is the author of *Walking the Labyrinth* (Main Street Rag, 2022) and the forthcoming chapbook, *Starter Mothers* (Finishing Line Press). Her poems have received awards from *Crosswinds Poetry Journal*, *Paterson Literary Review*, *Oberon Poetry Magazine* and the Robinson Jeffers Tor House and have been published in many other journals. Wax is a rabbi who walks labyrinths in the Bronx, New York, and the Northern Berkshires of Massachusetts. She can be found at www.pamelawax.com.

Scott Wiggerman is an Albuquerque author with three books of poetry, *Leaf and Beak: Sonnets*, *Presence*, and *Vegetables and Other Relationships*; and the editor of several volumes, including *Wingbeats: Exercises & Practice in Poetry* I & II. He is a member of the Texas Institute of Letters, and a frequent workshop instructor, especially in poetic form.

John Sibley Williams is the author of eight poetry collections, including *Scale Model of a Country at Dawn* (Cider Press Review Poetry Award), *The Drowning House* (Elixir Press Poetry Award), and *As One Fire Consumes Another* (Orison Poetry Prize). A twenty-six-time Pushcart nominee, John has won numerous awards, including the Wabash Prize for Poetry, Philip Booth Award, Phyllis Smart-Young Prize, and Laux/Millar Prize. He founded the Caesura Poetry Workshop series and serves as editor of *The Inflectionist Review*.

Charles Wilkinson's poetry collections include *The Snowman and Other Poems* (Iron Press), the pamphlet *Ag & Au* (Flarestack, 2013), and *The Glazier's Choice* (Eyewear, 2019). He lives in Wales, where he is heavily outnumbered by members of the ovine community. More information about his work can be found at his website: http://charleswilkinsonauthor.com.

Christie Max Williams' debut poetry collection, *The Wages of Love*, won the William Meredith Poetry Prize. He has worked as an actor and director in California, New York, and Connecticut. He also worked as a fruit vendor in Paris, a salmon fisherman in Alaska, a consultant on Wall Street, a writer for the National Audubon Society, and in leadership posts for non-profit organizations in whose causes he believes. He co-founded and for many years directed The Arts Café Mystic, which is in its 28th year of presenting programs featuring readings by America's best poets.

Avery Yoder-Wells is a trans, queer poet studying creative writing. Their work can be found in the *Portland Review*, *Mausoleum Press*, *VIBE*'s "bellyful" folio, *bs/ws*, and elsewhere. They lurk on Twitter at @averyotherwise.

Connecticut Poetry Society

Join the **Connecticut Poetry Society**, a state-wide community of poets dedicated to the promotion and enjoyment of poetry. CPS has a long tradition of excellence in publishing work of national and international, as well as Connecticut poets. Our mission is to encourage a community devoted to poetry through chapter meetings, education, and events. You do not need to be a resident of Connecticut to join.

Reap the benefits of CPS membership!

*Free copy of *Connecticut River Review*, a celebrated national poetry journal
*Quarterly CPS Newsletter of current poetry news and events
*Local Chapters for workshop and critique
*Annual Poetry Blast and open mic
*Annual Summer Picnic and open mic
*Annual contests
*Poets on Poetry educational presentations
*ConneCTions poetry readings and workshops featuring nationally-recognized poets
*Publicity for publications, readings, workshops
*Opportunity to publish poems on CPS website

Visit our website at ctpoetry.net

Join electronically via our website, or send your name, address, email address, phone, and check for dues ($30 individual, $15 student) made out to CPS to:

CPS Membership
311 Shingle Hill Road
West Haven, CT 06516.

Your membership is renewable in April – National Poetry Month!

Connecticut Poetry Society is a 501c3 organization. Member of The National Federation of State Poetry Societies (NFSPS)

Submission Guidelines for *Connecticut River Review*

Connecticut River Review, a national poetry journal, accepts submissions from February 1 through April 15.

Electronic submissions only:
https://connecticutriverreview.submittable.com/

Full guidelines can be found on the CPS website and the Submittable page.

What to send:

• Send up to three (3) original, previously unpublished poems on no more than four (4) pages in a single Word or pdf document, starting each poem on a separate page. Poems posted on social media or on personal blogs are considered previously published.

• We prefer Times New Roman font, 12 points, and left-aligned, unless formatting is part of the poem.

• Include a brief third-person bio of no more than 75 words in the cover letter section of the submission form.

• We accept simultaneous submissions. However, please notify us immediately if your work is accepted elsewhere. To withdraw part of your submission, contact us via the Messages function on Submittable. If you withdraw using the Withdraw button on Submittable, we will consider your entire submission withdrawn.

• Please submit only once during each reading period. Additional submissions during the same submission period will not be read. Upon publication: You will receive one copy of the journal in which your work is published.

Ordering Connecticut River Review

Connecticut River Review is priced at $15. Shipping and handling is $3.50. You can get more copies by mail by sending a check made out to CPS (or Connecticut Poetry Society) to:

CRR
9 Edmund Place
West Hartford, CT 06119

Be sure to clearly state where your order should be sent. *Connecticut River Review* is also available through amazon.com. Libraries and other institutions can order *CRR* through Ingram.

CPSIA information can be obtained
at www.ICGtesting.com
Printed in the USA
JSHW021928280722
28581JS00002B/17